'A Crayon up her Nose'

'A Crayon up her Nose'

The story of a typical village school,
told through the school logbooks,
over one hundred years

John Keble Primary School,
Hursley, Winchester, Hampshire
1863-1963

Compiled by Linda Hewett

ISBN 978-0-9568377-0-7

Printed and bound by CPI Antony Rowe Limited, Chippenham

Contents

Before we begin...

Atime of 'Fun and Freedom' – that's how I sum up my days at Hursley School in the 1950's. I discovered a love of writing and a life-long hatred of milk. I played conkers, 'two-ball', rounders and handstands. I climbed trees, played marbles and hopscotch. My friend Margot Tear and I made badges for our 'Jennings and Darbishire Club' (inspired by an Anthony Buckeridge radio series on BBC 'Children's Hour') – all in the special mix that was 'school'.

My younger brother Martyn and I lived at the top end of Chandler's Ford, which in the 1950s was within the catchment area for Hursley School. We travelled on a green Hants & Dorset double decker bus, number 46, and as we rumbled down the hill from

The metal railings by the shrubbery.

Ladwell, we'd scan the playground, hoping not to spot the dreaded dentist's caravan lurking menacingly in the playground. Martyn has kindly contributed his memories of this, near the end of chapter 12.

I loved my time at Hursley School and I wanted it to go on forever. But the 11-plus marked a sea change. I remember standing on the playground in those final summer term days in 1955, gazing out over the fields towards Ladwell, hot tears on my cheeks, suddenly aware that from now on life would be very different. I would be expected to grow up and would no longer be allowed to hang upside down on the metal railings by the school shrubbery, showing my knickers.

I'd love to go back and talk to my 11 year-old self, to tell her that one day in the next century she will be living in this village that she loves so much and be inspired to investigate the first 100 years in the life of her Primary School.

Introducing the logbooks

In front of me sits the earliest of the Hursley Schools' logbooks, for the Girls' School, started in 1863.

Before we turn to the entries, here on the first page, the official requirements and purposes of a school logbook are set out:

'In every school receiving annual grants, the managers must provide out of the school funds, a Diary or Logbook.

It must be stoutly bound and contain not less than 300 ruled pages.

The principal teacher must make, at least once a week in the Logbook, an entry which will specify ordinary progress, and other facts concerning the school and its teachers, such as dates of withdrawals, commencements of duty, cautions, illness etc.

No reflections or opinions of a general nature are to be entered in the Logbook.

The summary of the Inspectors' Report and any remarks made upon it by the Education Department ... must be copied verbatim into the Logbook.'

These pages, fragile in places, filled with fading copperplate handwriting, tell the fascinating story of daily and sometimes weekly happenings, building improvements, inspections, lessons taught, school visitors, illnesses, absences and punishments.

We read about 'Maying' – a May Day tradition described in chapter 13 – potato picking, blackberrying and haymaking, activities that provided a welcome respite from the daily tedium of school. Even a pouring wet day or a snowstorm were an excuse for a day off. In the nineteenth century, school was a world where the cane, the Dunce's Cap and slates were the norm.

In order to show which logbooks the extracts are from, I have used initials as follows:

(B) The Boys' School from 1866 to 1907.
(G) The Girls' School from 1863 to 1884.
(I) The Infants' School from 1875 to 1900.
(GI) When the Girls and Infants were in the same school from 1899 to 1906.
(N) When the schools were amalgamated and known as the Hursley National School from January 1907.
(JK) When the school moved into a new building, part of the present school building, in 1927.
(PS) When the school changed from an 'All Standard School' up to 13 year-olds and became a Primary School for 5 to 11 year-olds, from 1953 to the present day.

In the pages that follow, the logbook extracts tell their story.

I have also included several anecdotes from ex-pupils, which help to paint the picture of school life. I am indebted to all the individuals and sources listed in the acknowledgements, for their help in providing background information to set this story in its historical context. Wherever possible I have checked for factual accuracy but am open to correction if mistakes are found.

Introducing the Victorian education system

Before 1870, education was mainly for the upper and middle classes. Learning was for wealthy families, where it would begin with a governess. Boys might then move on to public school, girls continuing at home with the governess.

At first, attending school in England was voluntary. Many poor children were kept at home so they could go to work to help with the family income. There is evidence of this happening in Hursley, with haymaking, hop picking, stone and acorn collecting keeping children away from school.

In 1870 a law was passed requiring schools to be built for all children from 5 to 10 years but attendance was still voluntary, until 1880, when it became compulsory. Children could leave school at 10 years old unless they had a poor attendance record.

In 1893 the leaving age was raised to 11, to 12 in 1899 and in 1914 it was raised to 14, although special permission could sometimes be given to leave at 13.

The pattern of education in the Hursley schools in the last century was similar to that in many rural church schools. The school day began at 9 a.m. and the morning finished around noon when children could walk home for dinner, sometimes more than a mile, returning for afternoon school until 5 p.m.

The 'Three Rs' were taught daily – 'Reading, 'Riting and 'Rithmetic. Spelling and copy writing were particularly important and some geography and history were taught once a week. Sewing and knitting were included for all – even the boys were taught how to knit.

Religious instruction – sometimes referred to as the fourth 'R' – was taught daily in the Hursley schools, usually by the vicar, and church attendance during school hours was frequent. Passages from the Bible and prayer book were learnt by heart and recited in unison, even by the youngest children, who often remained ignorant of the meaning of the old-fashioned, archaic language.

From 1872, the government established 6 'Standards' in all schools, once a child had moved up from the Infants' classes. Standard 1 was for the youngest and Standard 6 for the 13 year-olds. However, as you read the logbook entries you will sometimes find the top two classes referred to as 'First Class' or 'Second Class' rather that 'Standard 5' or 'Standard 6'. This can be a little confusing...

At the end of every academic year, in March, the teacher or the Inspector gave exams in the 'Three R's'. If a child did not reach the required 'Standard' he would be kept down. As a result, some children never progressed beyond the first Standard.

In the next chapter we discover that during the last century there was more than one school in Hursley.

1

How many schools were there in Hursley?

THERE were four schools in Hursley during the last century – the Infants' School, the Girls' School, the Boys' School and the amalgamation of all these to form the National School in 1907, which was renamed the John Keble Memorial School, in 1927.

Sir William Heathcote's mother funded the first schools – the Boys' School and the Girls' School – in 1833. Sir William (1718 –1888) and his wife lived in Park House on the Hursley estate and were great benefactors to the village, taking an interest in everyone's welfare. All homes in Hursley were owned by Park House and rented to the estate workers. The Heathcotes funded the upkeep of these homes, and estate employees carried out the work.

In 1862, schools began to receive government grants according to their attendance

A group of estate workers... not forgetting the cat...

records and exam results. Four shillings a year was allocated for each child with a satisfactory attendance record. An extra eight shillings was given if the child passed the exams in reading, writing and arithmetic, before moving up into the next Standard.

The teachers' salaries also depended on the children's performances – in other words, they were 'paid by results'. In 1912 a head teacher would earn £80-£200 a year (£8,000-£19,000 a year today) and an assistant teacher, from £30-£50 a year, (about £3,000 in today's money.)

To encourage good attendance, Lady Heathcote awarded prizes for regular attendance and 'good conduct' and she was a frequent and welcome visitor at the schools.

The Girls' School was started in what became the modern day Committee Room, part of the village hall. It is still possible to see the marks on the brickwork where the children sharpened their slate 'pencils'.

The first entry in the logbook for the Girls' School *(G)* is May 18th 1863. The Schoolmistress was Miss Lucy Lampet.

She was the Schoolmistress for 44 years and lived at 'Culvers', number 37 on the Main Road in Hursley.

May 18th 1863 (G)
'An exceedingly rough and windy day, consequently very few children at school. Taught almost entirely collectively, having only seventeen children.'

From 1875 the Infants were educated separately in The Old Lodge, attached to the Girls' School building.

July 2nd 1875 (I)
'Infant School taken charge of by Carlotte Colson, ex-pupil and Provisionally Certificated. Average attendance Boys 22 and Girls 18.'

In 1877 a room in a cottage adjoining the Girls' School was set aside for the 'babies'.

In 1878 the logbook gives a list of the thirty-one children present for the annual visit by the HMI (Her Majesty's Inspector) to the Infants' School in March of that year.

'Frederick Earle, Andrew Mason, Edward Hayes, Humphrey Hancock, Frank Hawkins, Frederick Batten, George Mason, William Coffin, George Knight, Walter Callan, Samuel Down, Alfred Waterman, Arthur Coffin, Thomas Jackson, Gilbert Phillips, Christopher Witcher, William Bradley, Charles Batten, Alfred Browning, Harry Gear, Harry Bradley, Charlotte Beavis, Emily Richards, Emma Butler, Maude Bunce,

This picture of Lucy is displayed in school today, with the following dedication:
'In loving memory of Lucy Lampet, headmistress of Hursley Girls' School March 1st 1862-August 1st 1906'
'As poor, yet making many rich; as having nothing and yet possessing all things.'

Beatrice Phillips, Florence Clarke, Fanny Earle, Mary Down, Laura Wilson, Francis Hancock.'

The Boys' School building was originally a 17th century stable, established as a school in 1833, again courtesy of Mrs Heathcote. The building is now used as a Masonic Hall. The Schoolmaster lived in the house next to the school, and it was used for this purpose until 1987, when it was sold as a private home.

The first entry in the Boys' School logbook is September 3rd 1866, 3 years after the Girls' School.

September 3rd 1866
'Henry Plumridge, Schoolmaster. Opened with 33 scholars.'

Mrs Warr, Head teacher from 1953-1976, was the last teacher to live in the schoolhouse.

The Boys' School and the schoolhouse in 2010.

2

Word building and 'pieces of wood'

Reading, the first of the 3 R's, was taught to the whole class at the same time. The teacher stood in front, pointing to letters or words on the blackboard with a 'pointer' and the children would read these in unison. They were encouraged to read the Bible but this was often too difficult for them, so 'reading primers' (reading books) were introduced, with religious themes and morals to the stories.

A primer was intended to last for a year, so any quick readers would be very frustrated. If a primer was finished too early, the poor child would read it over and over, until everyone in the class was ready to go on to the next book.

December 6th 1878 (G)
'First Class began reading 'The Merchant of Venice' this week.'

First Class refers to the oldest children and Second Class to the younger ones.

November 4th 1881 (G)
'Tuesday being All Saints' Day the children did work in the afternoon and had a story read to them.'

It's interesting that having 'a story read to them' was recorded as an unusual event.

February 24th 1882 (I)
'Began using The Infant Reader with the First Class.'

March 17th 1882 (I)
'HMI Inspection 35 children.
The First Class read words of 2 syllables, wrote words of 1 syllable and worked addition and subtraction sums as far as 10's.
The Second Class added units, pointed words of 1 syllable from a reading book and wrote numbers as far as 10's.'

October 5th 1883 (I)
'Began teaching the babies how to form the letters of the alphabet by means of pieces of wood.'

Letter shapes were formed on the desks using strips of wood and the children would trace over the shapes with their fingers.

May 15th 1896 (B)
'Word building has been introduced.'

September 24th 1897 (B)
'Received some new Standard 2 reading books and object lesson sheets.'

'Object lessons' are explained in chapter 6.

February 18th 1902 (GI)
HMI Inspection
'He advised that some new pictorial reading sheets should be used in the Infants' room and suggested more variety in the way of teaching Arithmetic. More oral lessons should be given in Geography instead of depending entirely on reading lessons for this subject.'

The children read about other countries in their primers but received little or no extra explanation about geography or history from the teacher.

3

Copybooks, slates and 'a grievous stumbling block'

MANY Hursley villagers were illiterate, which was the norm for the time. The vicar, Rev John Keble, was particularly concerned that couples coming to be married were only able to 'make their mark'. He was keen that the village children should be taught to write and to read, with special emphasis on reading the scriptures.

The teaching of writing relied on the children copying examples from the blackboard, first onto slates and later into copybooks using pen and ink. They were not allowed to develop their own handwriting style and 'Blotting your copybook' resulted in a punishment, even the cane.

Children were not allowed to write with their left hands and were punished if they did so. Work on paper was not introduced until the 1860's, when it became less expensive, due to the excise duty on paper being abolished by Gladstone in 1861.

Slates were like small blackboards, and sharpened pieces of slate were used as 'pencils.' The children would clean their slates by spitting on their sleeve and rubbing out their work, unless a piece of rag was provided. They sharpened their slate pencils on the brickwork of the building.

Spelling was taught by the constant repetition of the order of the letters, in unison. The teacher would dictate words and sentences for the children to write down, often using passages from the Bible. Very often the children did not understand the meanings of the words they were asked to spell.

April 14th 1865 (G)
'Spelling still a grievous stumbling block to many.'

October 2nd 1866 (G)
'Gave the Second Class some copying to do while I gave a Scripture lesson to the First Class.'

March 24th 1871 (G)
'Tried a new plan for correcting bad spelling in Second Class, giving them all lists of words to learn with their meanings, as in old fashioned times.'

June 22nd 1877 (G)
'The girls, 5 in number, who have passed the 6th Standard are employed in Map Drawing while the First Class are writing.'

July 23rd 1880 (B)
'The Standard 2 boys are rather bad writers on the average.'

December 3rd 1880 (B)
'The school is rather dark now. The school is frequently so dark that the work in copybooks and on paper and on slates is almost an impossibility.'

I have researched the issue of lighting in the schools and, as far as I can tell, no artificial lighting was utilised until November 1924, when two lamps were provided for the schoolroom.

March 5th 1884 (G)
'Alice Gradidge failed in spelling as she always has done and probably always will.'

October 28th 1892 (B)
'Lately I have noticed a great improvement in the writing throughout the school which is doubtless owing to copies I have been setting on the blackboard.'

December 17th 1897 (B)
'The room has been very dark this week and boys can scarcely see to write at 3 o'clock.'

September 24th 1901 (GI)
'Standards IV, V and VI have been working simple exercises in Grammar, chiefly with reference to the Conjunction and the Preposition.'

'The room has been very dark… the boys can scarcely see to write at 3 o'clock.'

4

'Still far from satisfactory'

Arithmetic was taught daily and mental calculations were considered very important. This was sometimes referred to as 'reckoning' or 'reckoning up' and this expression for 'adding up' can still be heard today, amongst the older generation. Multiplication tables were 'chanted' every day, sometimes in time to tambourines, to help the memory.

May 27th 1863 (G)
'Examined the third class and found many below the standard in Arithmetic.'

July 7th 1863 (G)
'Began to teach the second class the Reduction Of Weights and Measures. Only a few succeeded.'

October 5th 1863 (G)
'Admitted 3 children: Elizabeth Bunce age 10, Charlotte Self age 6 and Mary Witcher age 6. None of them too sharp at figures. Very quiet and orderly.'

December 10th 1863 (G)
'A few children in the Second Class began to learn multiplication by 2 figures.'

December 18th 1863 (G)
'Found the Arithmetic of the 2 Upper Classes still far from satisfactory.'

March 4th 1864 (G)
'The whole of the Second Class failed to work out a simple subtraction sum correctly.'

March 18th 1864 (G)
'Arithmetic still the weak point in all classes.'

February 23rd 1865 (G)
'Mrs Richards taught one child to write down figures up to thousands.'

March 1866 (G)
Inspector's Report
'The Arithmetic papers of the Higher Standards are hardly as good as I had expected.'

In 1867, paper, which had been expensive, began to be used instead of slates in the Girls' School. The tax on paper had been abolished in 1861.

May 29th 1867 (G)
'First Class worked sums on paper (without slates) with a fair result (2 exceptions.)'

June 3rd 1867 (G)
'Helped 2 little ones to count.'

An abacus was used for making calculations and some children became extremely quick with it.

October 7th 1867 (G)
'First Class received a blackboard lesson for the explanation of working sums in Long Measure.' (The measurement of length.)

March 8th 1872 (G)
'Work entirely on paper now till the Examination. This week have been going over the work of the last 3 months, in Arithmetic especially.'

Exams were held annually in March, the end of the academic year at this time. If the children did well, the school received a larger grant from the local authority.

April 12th 1872 (G)
'The girls of Standard 6 have been working hard at Decimals, as the New Code requires Fractions, Decimals and Proportion now.'

The government now specified the teaching requirements for each 'Standard' in each subject.

June 24th 1875 (B)
'Inspector's report.
There are too many failures in Arithmetic.'

September 12th 1875 (B)
'As Arithmetic is deficient in the school and mentioned in the Government Inspector's Report, the time given to drawing will be given to Arithmetic.'

Arithmetic was considered far more important than drawing. Arithmetic was tested in the end of year examinations whereas drawing was not.

September 25th 1878 (B)
'Standard 5 boys are very weak at Reduction of Money. Some of them could not bring shillings and pence to farthings.'

April 23rd 1880 (G)
'Standard 4 have worked examples of Reduction in Avoirdupois and Troy Weight, in Time and Length and have begun Square Measure.'

Troy Weight was a system of measuring weight, where 12 ounces made a pound. This must have been confusing for the children, who had to calculate in Avoirdupois also, the Imperial System of weight, where 16 ounces made a pound.

March 5th 1883 (G)
'Example of Arithmetic problem in the examination of March 5th 1883, attempted by few or none:

'If herrings are ¾d (3 farthings) each, how many dozen could be bought for half a guinea, half a crown and nine pence?' '

May 16th 1892 (B)
'I have found great benefits from introducing Arithmetic Books in the Upper Standards.' (11-12 year-olds.)

December 13th 1895 (I)
'Children did tambourine drill to their tables.'

Drill is explained in chapter 19.

There are no further interesting references to Arithmetic until this one, by head teacher Mrs Warr, 65 years later, introducing a new method of teaching number called 'The Cuisenaire Method.'

October 25th 1960 (JK)
'I attended a meeting at Weeke County Primary School at which Miss Bradbourne spoke on the Cuisenaire Method of teaching number.'

A Belgian, Georges Cuisenaire, invented this method in the 1950s. The children used boxes of coloured wooden rods to demonstrate fractions and the four 'rules' of number. 'Cuisenaire maths', as it was known, became very fashionable in Primary Schools during the 1960's and 70's. It is still possible to buy boxed sets today and these are sometimes used in Home Schooling.

This Victorian abacus can still be seen in John Keble School.

5

'A case of lamentable ignorance'

UNTIL the 1920's there was little understanding by teachers or parents that children learn at different rates. A child who fell behind could be punished and often cruelly humiliated by having to sit on the Dunce's Stool and wear the Dunce's Cap. If a child failed to learn it was considered to be his fault for being inattentive or naughty. Children were not encouraged to ask questions. However, some efforts were made in the Hursley Schools to help those children who were falling behind.

With large classes it was necessary to teach everyone at once. There was no provision to teach small groups who needed further help or to extend the brighter children. Sometimes the teacher would give her time after school to give extra help to the ones who needed it or she would give them extra reading help in a needlework lesson when the rest of the children could get on without her for a while.

October 19th 1863 (G)
'Admitted Mary Chalk, a child who has been unavoidably kept from school for years to take care of younger children and is consequently deplorably backward in everything.'

May 25th 1865 (G)
'Discovered a case of lamentable ignorance and kept the child after school to try to teach her better.'

January 30th 1866 (G)
'Took a quarter of an hour from the needlework time to hear some backward readers.'

March 27th 1874 (G)
'Examined Standards I, II and III. A few shaky ones in each Standard at present and 'shaky' is their normal condition.'

June 26th 1874 (G)
'Bestowing extra care on backward children has been the work of the week.'

February 11th 1876 (G)
'A few dunces in each class retard progress.'

November 3rd 1882 (B)
'The Fourth Standard boys are very stupid and backward and are a great trouble. They appear to get worse instead of better.'

May 23rd 1884 (B)
'The Second Standard boys scarcely know any of their tables and are rather backward.'

June 13th 1884 (B)
'The First Class boys are not very successful in map-drawing – most of them have not the slightest idea how to proceed.'

October 6th 1899 (G)
'The Mistress had 3 backward scholars of Standard Four to give individual attention to each.'

June 28th 1908 (N)
'Winifred Harper was admitted today. She is 7 years old and has never been to school, neither does she know a single letter of the alphabet.'

May 5th 1924 (N)
'Backward children in Arithmetic and English to be given extra work during the Drawing Lesson.'

Unfortunately, when you were 'behind' in the 3 R's, the only way you could receive extra help was to miss some of the more enjoyable activities.

6

'Porous bodies, stinging nettles and the Newfoundland dog'

The area of the Victorian curriculum known as 'Object Lessons' is intriguing. The teacher gave a lesson on, say, rice, explaining how and where it was grown, its use and how to cook it. The children then wrote down what they had learnt or told the teacher what they could remember.

Very often no pictures were available to show the children what the teacher was talking about. It must have been extremely difficult for the teacher to describe a camel or a Newfoundland dog to the class, with no illustrations to help.

The diversity of these object lessons is quite curious. They seem to have been roughly divided into categories: crops, nature study, foods, household objects, animals and occupations.

Here are 20 of the 90 object lessons taught in the Infants' School between 1882 and 1900.

- chalk
- salt
- tapioca
- cotton
- gloves
- coal
- lead
- stinging nettle
- cleanliness
- umbrella
- camel
- whale
- crocodile
- ostrich
- the Newfoundland dog
- reindeer
- carthorse
- cuckoo
- plum pudding
- a railway station

At an inspection of the Infants' School in March 1890, it was noted that 'Some picture cards to illustrate the Object lessons should be supplied.'

June 20th 1890 (I)
'Put up 6 new pictures this week. Subject – trades. Gave a lesson on the baker.'

June 27th 1890 (I)
'Gave a lesson on the shoemaker.'

October 4ᵗʰ 1895 (I)
'A very wet day. Lessons given on the coat and the umbrella.'

September 4ᵗʰ 1896 (B)
'Object lessons given on 'porous bodies' and 'sponges.'
Several boys sent home this morning as they were wet through.'

March 12ᵗʰ 1897 (B)
'Taught the boys 'God save the Queen' and gave an Object lesson on The Union Jack.'

October 31ˢᵗ 1901 (GI)
'Lower division had an Object lesson on clothes pegs in connection with 'Domestic Economy Lessons on Washing.' '

7

Patchwork, 'drill' and rope brushes

The girls were prepared for their household duties by learning to sew, knit, repair their clothes and cook. Boys were also taught to knit and sew.

Many girls would leave school at thirteen to go into service. Country girls were considered by prospective employers to be more adaptable and manageable than city girls, so were much sought after as domestic servants. Lady Heathcote from Park House kept a list of suitable Hursley girls and there was much competition for a place on her list.

A housemaid would earn £10-£16 a year in 1880 (around £1,000 in today's money) with a half-day holiday on Sundays. Uniform, meals and accommodation were provided, so she would be able to send money home to help her family. 'Service' was the largest source of employment for girls and women at this time.

Workhouse girls were not considered suitable for service as they wouldn't be used to handling expensive or delicate china and, sadly, were thought of as 'stupid.' For more information about the Hursley workhouse, see chapter 12.

April 11th 1865 (G)
'Three girls kept after school to finish some needlework which had been badly done and consequently taken out.'

March 10th 1876 (G)
'Miss Worthington began teaching darning.'

April 28th 1876 (G)
'Mrs Young (vicar's wife) has been instructing the girls in patching.'

Here are two of the tasks that had to be completed for the girls' 1877 Needlework Inspection, one of several subjects to be inspected.

- Standard 4 – 'A square of calico of about 9 inches to be folded down, herringboned and a button-hole made'
- Standard 6 – 'To put on a patch, mark, name and darn.'

Copy of Inspector's report of the Girls' School for 1877.
'The school is in excellent order and the attainments are in many respects satisfactory. The Arithmetic, however, is inaccurate in too many cases and several failures have been caused by slight mistakes. The knowledge of Geography is imperfect at present but the Needlework is well done.'

February 7th 1879 (G)
'Began teaching Standard 4 to cut out a frock body and each afterwards cut one for herself.'

July 2nd 1880 (I)
'Children began knitting cuffs to show at the Flower Show at the end of the month.'

October 4th 1881 (G)
'Standards 4, 5 and 6 read and learnt Chapters 4 and 5 of "Domestic Economy, Clothing and Washing."'

March 17th 1882 (I)
'HMI Inspection – 35 children present.
As well as showing their reading and writing skills to the Inspector – both boys and girls did sewing and knitting in the Inspector's presence.'

Eve of examination for March 17th 1882 (I)
'Part of First Class kept in to finish their needlework (the little frocks in Standard VI.) Needlework specimens arranged and marked for tomorrow's inspection.'

March 29th 1882 (G)
'Miss Young began a sewing class with the elder girls for missionary purposes.'

I have tried to find out if this particular 'Miss Young' was the vicar's daughter but it would seem likely, with the reference to 'missionary purposes'.

Inspector's Report March 1882 (G)
'The examination in English Literature and Domestic Economy was conducted on paper after the girls had recited a few lines of the poetry learnt.
  Standard 5 had to paraphrase a passage in which they all failed, having never done such a thing before.
  In Geography the examination was oral and confined to the British Isles.'

July 7th 1882 (I)
'Children commenced knitting cuffs and scarves. Knitting and needlework substituted for marching.'

Marching was part of the 'drill' lesson, the Victorian version of P.E. Drill was a series of stretches and exercises performed either indoors, by the sides of the desks, or outdoors, if the weather allowed. The aim was to improve the fitness, discipline and obedience of the so-called 'lower classes' and was based on military drill routines used to train army recruits.

Drill was performed all together, copying the teacher, who would stand in front of the class to demonstrate. Sometimes drums or tambourines were used to help keep everyone in time.

'Wands' and dumbbells were sometimes used. Wands were long wooden sticks, which the children would use in the exercises, imitating the rifles used in army training.

The children did not change their clothes for drill.

November 3rd 1882 (I)
'Children have begun a patchwork quilt.'

December 6th 1883 (I)
'Finished making strips for knitted petticoats and cuffs for Inspection.'

May 16th 1884 (G)
'Usual singing lesson omitted to give more time to learning some new needlework – setting out frills on pinafores.'

November 14th 1884 (G)
'Singing lesson omitted this afternoon to have as much daylight as possible for needlework.'

HMI Inspection March 26th 1886 (I)
'All the first and second division did needlework and knitting for the Inspector. The babies pulled threads out from pieces of carpet.'

September 26th 1890 (I)
'Three of the Second Class boys have mastered their knitting this week.'

June 11th 1891 (I)
'First Class commenced hemming handkerchiefs.'

February 15th 1895 (I)
'The babies have been employed in the afternoons threading beads.'

September 27th 1895 (I)
'Taught the First Class a new kindergarten occupation – making rope brushes.'

October 16th 1896 (I)
'The babies threaded needles and had a marble for every time they did it which made it a counting lesson also. The girls have done needlework every afternoon this week and no knitting as they are so backward in it.'

May 25th 1900 (G)
'Some of the elder girls have been employed in needlework time knitting comforts for the soldiers in South Africa, Mrs Bacon providing wool etc.'

The British army was fighting in the Boer War in South Africa. The aim of the war was for the British to control the valuable gold and diamond states of Traansvaal and Orange Free State, occupied by the Dutch (Boers), and to retain these states as part of the British Empire, which they succeeded in achieving.

October 30th 1911 (N)
'Needlework had to be discontinued this afternoon owing to gusts of wind blowing soot down the chimney.'

December 11th 1935 (JK)
'Demonstration of weaving given at 6.30 p.m. by senior girls. Public admitted with a view to promotion of an adult class. Fifteen adult names given, 3 men among them.'

8

'Happy England', 'The Graves of a Household' and the school choir

MUSIC and singing were a popular form of entertainment at home. Music was considered to be an 'accomplishment' for 'young ladies'. Singing songs in school helped with reading, discipline, recitation and learning by heart.

November 16th 1866 (G)
'Mrs Young and Miss Terry came to give a singing lesson to the two upper classes, a thing which has been neglected.'

June 21st 1876 (G)
'List of songs to be prepared for the Inspector
1. 'Stitch! Stitch!'
2. 'Happy England'
3. 'I love the sunny days of Spring'
4. 'The Whale'
5. 'That Fairy like music'
6. 'Little Daisy'

List of songs to be prepared for 1877
1. 'Far away, Far away'
2. 'Gathering Flowers'
3. 'Mariner, spread the sails'
4. 'A Song for the Times'
5. 'Laugh while you may'
6. 'Golden Slumbers'
7. 'Happy England'
8. 'Hail, all Hail!' '

July 1st 1881 (G)
'Miss Laidlaw, the Infants' Teacher, gave a singing lesson to the girls on Wednesday when they learned to sing 'The Graves of a Household'.'

May 16th 1884 (G)
'Usual singing lesson omitted to give more time to learning some new needlework – setting out frills on pinafores.'

November 14th 1884 (G)
'Singing lesson omitted this afternoon to have as much daylight as possible for needlework.'

March 17th 1925 (N)
'School closed. 30 children taken to the musical festival at Winchester. Marks obtained – Sight Singing 40%, Unison Song 80%, Part Song 75%'

March 11th 1926 (N)
'The Hursley School Choir – thirty voices – assisted at the Hursley Choral Society concert giving the 6 songs they have prepared for the Winchester Musical Festival.'

March 20th 1926 (N)
'Choir entered for the Musical festival.
Sight Reading 70%, Unison Song 87% and 78%, Two part Song 83%, Folk Song 88%.
Total 406 out of 500.
Third in each class.'

9

School 'pence'

SCHOOLS were paid for by government grants from 1862. However, the amount was not always sufficient, and fees, known as 'pence' were charged. If there was more than one child in school from the same family, the fee was reduced. Wages were low and some families were unable – or in some cases, unwilling – to pay. Parents preferred to send their child to work for a few extra pence rather than pay money to the school. A labourer's wages were roughly 3s 9d a week – £9 a year – in 1900. (£900 today.) Half a loaf of bread cost 9d and a quart of milk (two pints) cost 5d.

The logbooks show that if a family couldn't afford the 'pence', they might move their child to a smaller school, which would be less expensive to equip so the 'pence' were less. These weekly fees were abolished in 1891.

Schools received a larger grant for higher numbers of pupils attending so a careful note of attendance figures was always made in the logbook, to show the inspector.

March 16th 1876 (B)
'Alfred Spreadbury gone to a small school in Compton, partly because unable to pay the school fees here.'

May 6th 1881 (I)
'Lady Heathcote says Infants to pay 2d a week.'

June 24th 1881 (G)
'Four children have left the school, in one case because the fees were raised to tuppence (2d) weekly.'

March 22nd 1883 (B)
'The managers have decided that 2d a week shall be the payment after the holidays in place of 3d to all boys who have a brother or sister at school with them.'

April 13th 1883 (B)

'The alteration in the payment from 1d to 2d and 3d has caused one or two boys to leave, Arthur Callen being one.'

March 1902 (B)

'The sum of £5 was allotted to this school to maintain the present charge for salaries.'

10

Beef tea, barley water and boiled potatoes

L ADY Heathcote realised how important it was for girls to learn to cook economically and healthily. She initiated the setting up of cookery lessons and went to the trouble of finding a certificated (qualified) teacher for this purpose. She often attended the lessons, to supervise. These lessons would not only enable the girls to help their mothers at home but would also prepare them for when they left home to go into service or, one day, to marry. It appears from the logbooks that some, if not all, of these special lessons took place on a Saturday.

November 3rd 1877 (G)
'A class for cookery established by Lady Heathcote for the benefit of the pupil teachers and elder girls. It is held in the babies' room where there is a suitable kitchen range and is under the superintendence of Miss Wells of Winchester, a first class certificated teacher from South Kensington.'

'Pupil teachers' are explained in chapter 18.

November 10th 1877 (G)
'Cookery lesson on soups – Lady Heathcote present.'

November 17th 1877 (G)
'Cookery instruction today on Cookery for the Sick e.g. easier ways of making beef tea and barley water.'

December 7th 1877 (G)
'Cookery class on Saturday by Miss Wells – baked fish, shepherd's pie, plum pudding. This was the last of the 'demonstrations' by Miss Wells – the practical part being to follow.'

Miss Wells showed the girls what to do. Then they cooked by themselves the following week.

December 14th 1877 (G)

'Cooking lesson given to First Class by Miss Wells. The pupils did everything themselves and succeeded very well. The dinner was given to four sick or poor people.'

January 12th 1878 (G)

'Practical cooking lesson by Miss Wells. Soups, vegetables and macaroni.'

January 19th 1878 (G)

'Cooking lesson – Course for a sick room – beef tea in two ways, barley water and arrowroot.'

Arrowroot was similar to corn flour and was used to make a pudding. It was easily digestible and nourishing for convalescents. It would be made into a blancmange by mixing to a paste with a little water or milk and then adding a pint of boiling water or milk. Arrowroot was also suitable for feeding to babies.

January 26th 1878 (G)

'Cookery lesson – roast mutton, semolina pudding and boiled potatoes.'

February 2nd 1878 (G)

'The last of a series of lessons on Artisan cooking by Miss Wells – shepherd's pie and plum pudding – which was given by Lady Heathcote to the girls who cooked.'

November 21st 1911 (M)

'Miss Morrison from the County Council commenced 'Combined Domestic Subjects' with eighteen girls at a cottage adjoining the Audit Room.'

April 15th 1920 (N)

'A series of lessons in cookery began this afternoon in the Scout Hut.'

April 3rd 1925 (N)

'Cookery Class A

Eighteen girls started Cookery class today:

Beatrice Ricketts, Dorothy Heath, Gwendoline White, Lily Ireland, Mary Velly, Edith Jones, Bessie Perrin, Rose Bacon, Rose Earles, Freda Giles, Mabel Knight, Gertrude Hayes, Ivy Sinsbury, Vera Dewey, Norah Williams, Iris Rimpton, V. Allard, Phyllis Snook.'

11

'The Sinful Lusts of the Flesh' and 'The Dead Doll'

RECITATION and repetition featured prominently in the school day. Rote learning was relied upon for tables in Arithmetic, and Bible and prayer book passages were memorised in scripture lessons. Even the under 7's were expected to learn Bible passages and the catechism by heart, despite not understanding all the words.

June 8th 1863 (G)
'First class examined by the Rev John Keble in Holy Scripture.'

John Keble was vicar of Hursley from 1835-1866. He gained a double first degree at Oxford at eighteen and was a tutor at Oriel College Oxford from 1818-1823. Keble College Oxford was established in his memory in 1870. One of his students was Sir William Heathcote of Park House. In 1836 William asked Keble to come to Hursley as its priest. He was also rector of Otterbourne.

Keble published his book of poems, 'The Christian Year', in 1827. In 1848 he used the substantial profits from the sale of his book to rebuild Hursley church in a style more suited to his Anglo-Catholic beliefs.

He gave much of his time to the poor and sick in the village and paid special attention to the inhabitants of the workhouse, making regular visits. More details about the Hursley Union workhouse can be found in chapter 12.

He and his wife were very involved in the life of the schools, teaching the scriptures daily, sometimes in their home.

Charlotte Yonge – 1823-1901 – was a great friend of the Kebles. She was a historian and prolific novelist, writing 160 books. She was compared favourably with Jane Austen and was widely read and respected as one of the best-known writers in the world at the time.

She lived all her life in Elderfield House, on the Main Road in Otterbourne, and taught in the Sunday school for 71 years, from the age of 7.

Rev and Mrs John Keble with Charlotte Yonge in the vicarage garden in 1861.

June 9th 1863 (G)
'First class received a Scripture lesson from Mrs Keble.'

Sometimes Mrs Keble gave scripture lessons at her home, now known as the Old Vicarage, which was close to the Girls' School. Thomas Heathcote of Park House built the house in 1824 and it became the official vicarage in 1842. It was the Kebles' home from 1836-1866.

June 29th 1863 (G)
'St Peter's Day. The children had not time before the morning service to repeat the Gospel.'

July 9th 1863 (G)
'The First Class repeated a portion of the psalms, learnt as a home lesson for Thursday, generally not satisfactorily.'

October 26th 1863 (G)
'The First Class received a lesson on the Sin of Slander from the Rev John Keble.'

December 21st 1863 (G)
'The Third class strangely neglected repeating the lesson of the collect and the Gospel of the day and were kept after school to learn the collect.'

January 11th 1864 (G)
'I have chosen to carry the children through the history of the first 5 books of the Bible during the proposed long absence of the Vicar.'

Rev Keble travelled to Torquay and Penzance for a complete rest towards the end of 1864. He had suffered a small stroke and his wife was also in poor health. They later stayed in Bournemouth for a while to enjoy the benefits of the sea air.

March 21st 1864 (G)
'This being Holy Week will be a different character from an ordinary week. The children will attend morning service throughout the week.'

May 6th 1864 (G)
'Kept a Class after school for coming in from church in a disorderly manner.'

May 30th 1864 (G)
'The Rev John Keble came this morning to give a lesson to the First Class – subject – the 'Sinful Lusts of the Flesh.'

October 7th 1864 (G)
'Found the Third Class very scattered in their ideas about the history of Moses.'

October 28th 1864 (G)
'After church the children repeated pieces of poetry instead of the usual routine of lessons.'

February 3rd 1865 (G)
'Found on hearing the little ones repeat their catechism that many could not articulate 'Pontius Pilate' properly or had not been taught to do so.'

February 6th 1865 (G)
'Rev W. Richards came to give a lesson on the creed of Athanasian. Several late.'

March 1st 1865 (G)
'Mrs Richards heard the first class speak their psalms.'

March 20th 1865 (G)
'Kept 5 little girls, who came in late after prayers, to write the fourth commandment on their slates.'

September 15th 1865 (G)
'Discovered that one child, lately admitted, could not say the Lord's Prayer – kept her to learn it.'

February 15th 1866 (G)
'Psalms very nicely repeated today.'

March 12th 1866 (G)
'Several First Class girls kept to correct their dictation exercise which was very faulty today. Perhaps rather a difficult piece.'

October 29th 1866 (B)
'Rev Young takes scripture lessons twice a week.'

John Keble died on 29th March 1866. Rev Young took over from him as vicar.

December 14th 1866 (G)
'Classes 2 and 3 examined in church catechism. Little ones disposed to slur over the little words, otherwise tolerably perfect.'

January 17th 1867 (G)
'The whole of the First Class kept back to write their psalms on their slates having been most imperfectly repeated to Mrs Young.'

April 10th 1867 (G)
'Kept the whole school in for twenty minutes for coming in noisily from church.'

April 15th 1867 (G)
'Holy Week. The children go to church every morning.'

March 22ⁿᵈ 1869 (B)
'Children taken to church every day this week.'

February 7ᵗʰ 1870 (G)
'The Vicar came to teach First Class. He began going through the Book of Common Prayer.'

March 16ᵗʰ 1871 (G)
'Kept nearly all First Class for careless repeating of psalms.'

March 23ʳᵈ 1871 (G)
'Psalms much better said today – last week's punishment was beneficial in effect so far.'

March 28ᵗʰ 1872 (G)
'School closed for two days. Tomorrow being Good Friday the work will be purely of a religious character.'

Evidence can be seen here of the sharpening of slate 'pencils' on the brickwork.

May 19ᵗʰ 1876 (G)
'Holiday for Ascension Day. Standard V said their recitation as a Holiday Treat.'

September 12ᵗʰ 1881 (G)
'The Sunday scholars all received a new dress, jacket and bonnet each in mourning for the Right Honourable Sir William Heathcote, the liberal patron of the schools in the parish.'

Sir William died in August 1881 after a long illness.

May 13ᵗʰ 1885 (I)
Diocesan Inspection report for the Infants.
'Old Testament – good, New Testament – good, Catechism and Liturgy – good, Repetition – good. Very effectively taught and well trained.'

February 15th 1895 (I)
'For the coming Inspection the poem to be learned for recitation is called 'The Dead Doll'.'

This seems a strange choice of poem for younger children.

April 26th 1895 (I)
'Thursday was Scripture Examination Day. Being a very wet morning, twenty-one children were absent.'

12

Bad feet, blackberries and beaters

B
AD weather, casual employment and illnesses accounted for many absences from school. All absences were required by law to be recorded in the logbooks as the schools' maintenance grants depended on the numbers present. The Attendance Officer was informed of any worrying situations and would visit the family.

In the nineteenth century and up to the 1920's, childhood diseases often resulted in deaths. Three out of ten babies would die before their first birthday and life expectancy for an adult was about sixty years. Most families had several children, fully aware that not all would survive beyond childhood.

Scarlet fever (sometimes referred to as scarlatina), measles and diphtheria were very serious. The first mass immunisations weren't available for diphtheria until the 1920s, for whooping cough until 1926 and for measles not until 1963. Scarlet fever epidemics were common and very much feared, as death could result.

May 18th 1863 (G)
'An exceedingly rough and windy day, consequently very few children at school.'

June 30th 1863 (G)
'A very thin attendance today. The children are kept at home either to assist or play in the hay fields.'

July 24th 1863 (G)
'One girl in the First Class, Emma Kitchen, has left for service this week.'

September 14th 1863 (G)
'Commenced school. Very few in attendance, the greater number being kept away to pick hops.'

There were hop gardens in Hursley in 1863. In 1880 they are referred to in the logbook as 'having been done away with'.

October 21ˢᵗ 1863 (G)
'Removed Eliza Fellett from the register in consequence of very irregular attendance.'

January 18ᵗʰ 1864 (G)
'A great many children came in late this morning – a usual circumstance on Mondays.'

January 26ᵗʰ 1864 (G)
'Four or five children absent till 10 o'clock to fetch soup from Park House.'

In very cold weather soup was sometimes provided by Lady Heathcote to help keep the children warm and healthy.

February 10ᵗʰ 1864 (G)
'Lady Heathcote made enquiries about Mary Trodd – a child who has been kept from school in consequence of having been sent home for disobedience.
Note: She was readmitted on February 22ⁿᵈ after being expelled ... with apologies and promises for future conduct. Lady Heathcote expostulated with her parents.'

May 9ᵗʰ 1864 (G)
'Took a child's name off the register – Jane Keel – wanted at home.'

Park House. Hursley

Published by J. Bailey & Co, Southampton. Copyright

Mothers often relied on their daughters to help at home, often looking after the younger children in the family, while their mothers worked in the fields.

June 15th 1864 (G)
'Attendance very thin indeed, some because their mothers are out haymaking and some have scarlet fever.'

September 26th 1864 (G)
'Lady Heathcote gave permission for several extra girls to be placed on her list until any vacancies occur.'

This is a reference to her list of girls suitable for service at Park House.

June 18th 1866 (G)
'A very wet day and consequently a very poor attendance – the worst scholars absent too.'

September 17th 1866 (G)
'Extremely poor attendance, most of the children being engaged in picking hops.'

July 29th 1867 (G)
'Attendance falling off considerably. Harvest work beginning.'

September 26th 1867 (G)
'Hop picking giving way to potato picking – desultory work.'

February 17th 1868 (G)
'A very thin attendance with so many away with coughs and colds. Some older sisters are away nursing them.'

October 21st 1868 (G)
'Few children present, acorn picking taking them away.'

Acorns were collected to provide extra food for the family pig, which was reared for its meat.

May 27th 1870 (G)
'Attendance not good this week – a few cases of scarlatina have caused a panic.'

February 7th 1871 (B)
'Charles and Herbert left school. Mother left the Union.'

Presumably she was now able to provide financially for her family so they were no longer destitute and able to leave the workhouse.

The Hursley Parish workhouse was established in 1828. In 1835 it became known as the Union workhouse, providing homes for the 'destitute poor' from Farley Chamberlayne, Otterbourne, Compton and Hursley.

The workhouse held thirty-three inmates at the census of 1881. A brick wall was built down the middle of the buildings, separating the men's side from the women's. There was a washhouse and lavatory on either side of this wall.

There were 4 'classes' of inmates and men and women were separated as follows:
- old and infirm men and boys over 7
- able-bodied men
- old and infirm women and girls over 7
- able-bodied women and children under 7.

Inspection reports of the time tell us the workhouse was well run and the occupants were reasonably well fed. In the 1881 census the master of the workhouse, George Readhead, is noted as being blind.

The following children were living in the workhouse in 1881:
Charles Batten (9), Frederick Batten (8), Amelia Bunday (4), Frank Bunday (5), Emma J. Butler (9), Henry Martin (12), James Martin (4) and Alice Purnell (10).

As the population in the area grew, a larger workhouse was needed, to include the destitute poor of Chandler's Ford. In 1900 the new workhouse, built close to Hursley Road in Chandler's Ford, was opened and the Hursley school children were taken to witness the opening ceremony. See chapter 13 for more about the new workhouse.

The original Hursley building was converted into 10 cottages for estate workers. In 1980 the site was sold and renovated to provide 6 charming private homes.

January 9th 1872 (G)
'Mistress away with a cold. First and Second classes came to her house once a day for instruction.'

November 8th 1872 (G)
'Two days of the Clothing Club Sale. This kept many at home so their mothers could be at the sale.'

Clothing Clubs were set up to help families save for new clothes for their children. This entry suggests that second-hand clothes may also have been collected and sold.

June 19th 1874 (G)
'Schoolmistress absent 2 days to consult an oculist. Work carried on by pupil teachers, aided by Rev and Mrs Young.'

The role of a 'pupil teacher' is explained in chapter 18.

July 30th 1874 (G)
'Gleaning began today.'

Gleaning was legally allowed for cottage dwellers in the nineteenth century. Leftover crops could be collected from the harvest fields for free, once the 'official' harvesting was finished.

October 23rd 1874 (G)
'Duties of Schoolmistress taken by Isabella Matilda Stanford, certificated teacher, in the temporary absence of the mistress through partial loss of sight.'

January 19th 1877 (G)
'Wet weather has very much thinned the younger part of the scholars – the distant ones being almost unable to face the watery lanes.'

It was not unusual for children to walk a mile or more to school.

February 9th 1877 (G)
'Attendance still poor, especially in the Little Class, whooping cough prevalent.'

Whooping cough often proved fatal for children at this time.

September 28th 1877 (G)
'Began school ten minutes late having been blackberrying with them in the dinner hour.'

May 17th 1878 (B)
'Bradley Alder away at work tying hop plants around the poles. He attends school very badly and consequently is rather backward in his work.'

May 20th 1879 (B)
'The Hants Yeomanry assembled out in the Park for drill. Many boys have absented themselves to witness the sight.'

The Hampshire Yeomanry Cavalry helped fight off the Zulus at Rorke's Drift in South Africa, in the Anglo-Zulu war in 1879. The troops assembled in the Park before embarking from Southampton. It would have been very exciting for the boys to watch them perform their drill.

July 11th 1879 (B)
'Earnest Webb away owing to bad feet.'

April 30th 1880 (B)
'Several boys away, helping remove the bark from the trees.'

I have been unable to discover why this was done.

May 28th 1880 (G)
'Sent home one child with whooping cough and two others absent with ringworm.'

September 13th 1880 (G)
'Much better attendance than is usual at this time, the hop gardens having been done away with.'

September 17th 1880 (G)
'Edith Earle, a Fifth Standard girl, leaves school for service in the village.'

September 17th 1880 (B)
'Sent A. Bone home as his head is covered in sores.'

October 8th 1880 (B)
'Batten obliged to stay away owing to his head being cut open with a hoop.'

January 10th 1881 (G)
'The weather has been so cold and snowy that attendance has fallen off very considerably.'

January 18th 1881 (G)
'A deep snow. Only 9 present. The vicar gave notice that the school must be closed. The parish is a scattered one, roads and lanes utterly impassable, the snow in places being many feet deep.'

March 4th 1881 (G)
'Four children away with ringworm, the worst cases coming from the Union.'
This refers to the Hursley Union workhouse.

September 30th 1881 (G)
'E. J. Wilson, a little scholar died.'

The funeral of a child would not have been an unusual event for the scholars to witness.

June 16th 1882 (I)
'Many children taking care of their smaller brothers and sisters while the mother goes hay-making.'

June 16th 1882 (I)
'Lady Heathcote has promised prizes to all those who attended over four hundred times during the last school year.'

June 30th 1882 (B)
'Attendance worse this week than it has been for years, only 18 present this afternoon. It does not appear of any use to write to the Attendance Officer as the law is totally ignored by some of the parents.'

November 3rd 1882 (I)
'Many children still absent on account of chilblains.'

September 11th 1883 (G)
'Several girls have left. Minnie Corbin in Standard 4, being over thirteen years of age, may legally do so.'

October 20th 1883 (G)
'Francis and Richard Hannah's family are leaving the village for Australia.'

Some emigrants to Australia at this time were offered passage money (fares) instead of Poor Relief but the logbook does not make it clear why this family emigrated.

December 14th 1884 (I)
'Only fifteen children present, it being a very wet day.'

February 4th 1887 (I)
'One little boy absent through a dog-bite.'

October 28th 1887 (B)
'Several boys irregular on account of acorns.'

February 17th 1888 (I)
'Attendance scanty owing to the inclement weather.'

November 19th 1889 (B)
'Many scholars absent being employed 'beating' for the shooters.'

Boys could earn a few pence by driving the pheasants out of 'cover', for the shoots held on the estate.

November 14th 1890 (I)
'The boys have been very irregular during the week owing to bad colds.'

February 13th 1891 (I)
'Walter Ward came to school for the first time since Christmas.'

November 11th 1892 (B)
'Attendance has suffered severely this week on account of diphtheria. Several boys have been told not to attend school.'

April 21st 1894 (B)
'Several boys are at work gathering stones from the meadows.'

October 19th 1894 (G)
'Edith Hayes left school for the winter months.'

January 4th 1895 (B)
'Bertie Bunney came back to school after being away for two months.'

April 26th 1895 (I)
'Thursday was the Scripture Examination Day. Being a very wet morning, twenty-one children were absent.'

May 1st 1896 (I)
'A whole holiday being May Day. Owing to the illness of so many children there was no May Queen this year.'

May 4th 1896 (I)
'7 children present.'

July 1st 1898 (B)
'The attendance is simply disgraceful. Boys are employed by a member of the District Council and for haymaking.'

May 25th 1900 (G)
'Attendance still greatly thinned by measles and several cases of ringworm of a very bad kind.'

Everyone helps with the haymaking in 1910.

September 28th 1900 (G)

'In consequence of the removal of the Union (Workhouse) to new premises at Chandler's Ford, the children have left our school today – this makes a considerable gap in our ranks.'

July 11th 1902 (B)

'Attendance has been very low indeed, no less than 9 boys being illegally employed the whole week.'

By law children were now to stay at school until they were thirteen. They were not allowed to be officially employed while still at school and employers could be fined.

July 31st 1902 (G)

'Three scholars have left the village in consequence of the death of their mother – Ethel, Frances and Emma Hicks.'

May 5th 1905 (G)

'The Managers, by order of the medical officer Dr Livingston, have closed the school for 3 weeks. Very few of the older scholars are attacked (measles) but they are not allowed to come to school if there is any case in their house.'

September 11th 1905 (G)

'Whooping cough has appeared amongst the little ones.'

October 2nd 1908 (N)

'Measles rapidly on the increase. Many absent through scarlet fever.'

March 29th 1911 (N)

'Albert Clark and Frank Carswell are both gone with their fathers to Southampton, simply to have ride in a wagon.'

November 24th 1915 (N)

One girl, who has been away from school throughout the school year suffering with St. Vitus' Dance, has just returned.'

St. Vitus' Dance is a symptom of rheumatic fever. Symptoms include jerky, uncontrollable movements similar to twitching. It is a more common condition in girls.

A 'motorcar' was a rare sight in the village in the 1920s.

October 2nd 1919 (N)
'A boy in the Infants Class, Rowland Cobb, in crossing the road near the school, was injured by a motorcar which passed over him. The child was entirely to blame.'

May 16th 1920 (N)
'Chicken pox around. And impetigo.'

Impetigo was the most common skin disease in children at this time. It could last 2 to 3 weeks. Touching a sufferer's skin or sharing towels or flannels very quickly spread the condition.

June 16th 1921 (N)
'Willie Coward, Standard I, age 7, was killed by the village bus near the King's Head. He was taking a message from his mother and slipped. The rear wheel passed over his head.'

August 2nd 1923 (N)
'Sixteen children are now excluded suffering from scarlet fever. All exercise books, pens etc. belonging to these children have been destroyed.'

"Scout" Motor Service Bus, to carry
1 Ton of Merchandise or 16 Passengers.

If scarlet fever was diagnosed, patients were sent to isolation hospitals and all their possessions were burnt. Children up to 8 years old were most susceptible.

September 10th 1923 (N)
'Stock is in such a state of confusion. The disinfecting necessitated the removal of all books for spraying.' See entry above.

January 15th 1925 (N)
'Weighing and measuring of whole school commenced.'

April 3rd 1925 (N)
'Attendance today very poor owing to many children taken by parents to the Hursley Point-to-Point races.'

Point-to-point races began in the 19th century and were originally called 'hunt races'. Their purpose was to keep the horses used for hunting fit during the non-hunting season, from February to May. All the riders were amateurs. Races were at least 3 miles long and involved jumping. There were about fifty point-to-points around the country in 1900.

September 9th 1925 (N)
'Dentist visited the school.'

March 5th 1926 (N)
'Nineteen absent all the week with flu, 4 in hospital.'

June 7th 1926 (N)
'Epidemic of German measles seems to be increasing.'

June 29th 1926 (N)
'School nurse called – reported case of Vera Allard blind in one eye.'

October 4th 1926 (N)
'Twelve children excluded for impetigo.'

October 29th 1926 (N)
'Whooping cough still severe.'

September 26th 1927 (N)
'Inspector Arnold, NSPCC, called to investigate a case of alleged cruelty. Child was interviewed and parents visited.'

September 2nd 1930 (JK)
'One of the Infants, Kathleen Perrin, suddenly left her older cousin and darted across the road at 3 p.m. at the close of school. She was knocked down by a motorcar and trailer and was run over by both vehicles but no wheel touched her. Dr reports nothing dangerous.'

October 9th 1931 (JK)
'Frances Salter, Head of School, Captain of Games, senior prefect, a brilliant scholar, left school on Friday October 9th to take up post of clerk at Aylwards wine merchants. Commenced work 12th October, taken ill same day, died on 15th, to be buried today. Headmaster attending funeral.'

February 24th 1933 (JK)
'Very heavy snow. Driver of bus for Farley children called at 11.45 to say that he couldn't guarantee negotiating the hills to Farley after 1 p.m.'

November 16th 1933 (JK)
'Letter received from Education Office to say that inspection of the home conditions of one of our families has recommended. The assistant (teacher) will no longer be

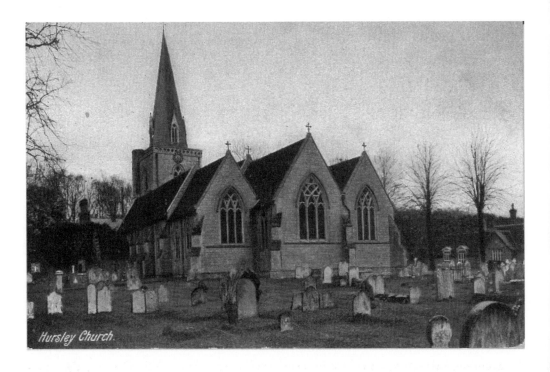

Hursley Church.

allowed to treat running sores on the children, as the parents' neglect is the cause. As they are borderline cases educationally, their attendance is a waste of time.'

November 23rd 1933 (JK)
'The children returned – examined – found fairly clean – few nits only.'

The school nurse checked children's heads regularly for head lice. They are wingless insects that live in clean or dirty hair and their eggs are called 'nits'. The way to remove them was to comb the hair very carefully with a fine-toothed comb. They don't jump and they are unable to survive away from the scalp. Nits are passed on by close contact with an infested head.

December 6th 1933 (JK)
'Some children found verminous – excluded.
Examined one boy – found legs covered with septic sores due to lack of elementary cleanliness. Parents indifferent. Dr sent child to parish nurse for treatment at home.'

February 8th 1934 (JK)
'Thirteen cases of whooping cough.'

February 23rd 1934 (JK)
'One girl still with nits in hair – excluded– two miles to walk home.'

January 15th 1935 (JK)
'One boy returned – head no cleaner. Told to get rid of them himself by combing.'

October 14th 1936 (JK)
'Two children still found with dirty heads, little attention had been paid. Mother asked to have nits pointed out. This was done. Parent then broke down. Fear of husband. Child was provisionally returned to classroom subject to future condition of head.'

October 15th 1936 (JK)
'Child excluded again, head still dirty.'

February 5th 1941 (JK)
'Inoculation against diphtheria of eighty-three children today.'

A vaccination programme for diphtheria was introduced in 1940. Diphtheria was a very common, serious and contagious illness and was the main cause of death in children. Nowadays it is very rare.

July 12th 1944 (JK)
'Frank Smith, 10 years old, fell from a tree in the shrubbery twenty-five minutes after school closed and badly lacerated his leg. He was taken to hospital.'

November 14th 1946 (JK)
'Dental Inspection of all children.'

January 10th 1947 (JK)
'The school bus conveying the Pitt children to school this morning was run into by an army lorry. Apparently only minor damage was sustained by one or two children. The teacher in charge, Miss Sloan, had a cut elbow and knee and a pair of stockings ruined. The children from Pitt arrived at school.'

May 13th 1948 (JK)
'Dental inspection of all children.'

March 15th 1950 (JK)
'Hearing of all 1938 and 1942 children tested by gramophone audiometer.'

November 24th 1950 (JK)
'At the end of the needlework lesson yesterday, the child coiling up the flex of the hot iron touched a girl on the left cheek with it, causing a burn about an inch long. The doctor says it may leave a scar.'

February 23rd 1951 (JK)
'A 9 year-old girl (Hutments, Hook Road, Chandler's Ford) who suffered very severe head injuries about 4 years ago saw another accident on her way to school. She was in the schoolyard at 5 to 9 just before the bell. At 9 a.m. she was missing and not found until 11.15 a.m. on the roof of the shed at her home, apparently mentally shaken. 3 p.m. – visit of Welfare Officer.'

June 28th 1951 (JK)
'Dental inspection followed by treatment until July 3rd.'

October 13th 1952 (JK)
'A girl admitted this morning, 9-10 years old, has not been in a school before and is living in tents at Pitt.'

July 3rd 1953 (JK)
'School dental surgeon held a clinic in caravan in school playground.'

Martyn Welch, brother of the author and Hursley School pupil from 1953-1959, describes the arrival of the dentist's caravan.

'I would feel my stomach knot as our double decker bus (Hants & Dorset No 46) approached the end of the road from Chandler's Ford and the school could be seen across the fields. The cause of my fear wasn't school as this was a happy experience for me – no, it was the dreaded sight of the white caravan parked at the Infants' end of the school. This was the school dentist and it was parked there so that the outlet from the caravan could be positioned over the drain next to the classroom's brick wall.

We boys would stand mesmerised as water and blood gushed into the drain at regular intervals, to be shortly followed by yet another terrified child stumbling from the door clutching their cheek. Inside was worse as we suffered horrendous pain at the claws of the evil white-coated devils lurking within. A filling was a brutal affair with only medical alcohol rubbed on a gum to supposedly alleviate the pain, which it failed stupendously to do. No injections in those days for young children.

It's taken me fifty five years since then to overcome my fear of the dentist, albeit still holding on to a strangely morbid fascination.'

January 28th 1954 (JK)
'Owing to the snow and treacherous conditions of the roads, attendance only sixteen this morning and seventeen this afternoon.'

February 1st 1954 (JK)
'Attendance still low. Farley transport not running. Pitt transport ran, no children on it.'

July 22nd 1955 (JK)
'Five year-old Eileen poked a crayon up her nose this morning. After consulting the doctor I sent her to hospital. It was removed there. Child returned to school.'

November 17th 1955 (JK)
'Nurse came to check up on certain children who she has found ill clad.'

February 9th 1956 (JK)
'Miss Smith, Senior Probation Officer, visited me this afternoon re – child who is on probation.'

January 6th 1958 (JK)
'Attendance not good owing to chickenpox.'

January 13th 1960 (JK)
'Heavy snow has fallen all day – transports left at 1.15 and 1.45. Children who use 46 bus left early.'

January 14th 1960 (JK)
'The Farley bus did part of the route this morning but only the Standon children came on it.'

13

'Maying', Morris dancing and a magic lantern

EXTRA holidays were always meticulously recorded in the logbooks. Confirmation services were popular with the scholars, as time off was usually given to attend them. Weddings, funerals, school 'feasts', May Day celebrations and even a visit to see the new Workhouse in Chandler's Ford, meant time off school.

September 23rd 1863 (I)
'A holiday, being the day of the Harvest Festival. The children had tea in the Park.'

April 4th 1864 (G)
'A Half Holiday as all sixteen girls went to the Park for tea and to receive prizes.'

June 13th 1864 (G)
'School Feast. Holiday in the afternoon. Tea on the vicarage lawn. Played in the Park till 8 o'clock.'

October 16th 1865 (G)
'The ordinary routine set aside – the day being a kind of festival in memory of the Consecration of the Church. Children had tea and a bun each in the schoolrooms.'

May 18th 1866 (G)
'A poor attendance today – the funeral of Mrs Keble. School hours rather interrupted in consequence.
Registers not marked till 2.20 as we witnessed the marriage of Miss Wilson, a former scholar here.'

Mrs Keble died only 6 weeks after the death of her husband.

December 20th 1866 (G)
'A few of the older girls stopped after school hours to make wreaths for the Church decorations.'

April 30th 1867 (G)
'Mrs Young and Mrs Terry came to help the children make their Maypole.'

January 9th 1868 (B)
'Holiday. Concert in schoolroom in evening.'

April 28th 1868 (G)
'Mrs Young came to hear the children sing their May Day songs.'

May 1st 1868 (G)
'Holiday. May Day treat at the vicarage.'

July 12th 1877 (G)
'School feast. A short service in the church at 2 p.m. with an address from the vicar. The children then went to Merdon Hills and had a delightful picnic tea, the little ones going in wagons. After tea Lady Heathcote gave rewards and prizes to every child who had been regular in attendance, successful in passing the Examination and otherwise deserving.'

April 8th 1880 (G)
'A holiday given by request of Miss Elsie Young, it being her wedding day.'

I have been unable to discover if Elsie was the Rev Young's daughter but I think it was likely, as a day's holiday was granted.

April 30th 1880 (G)
'Several of the little ones stayed away to pick flowers for their May Day garlands. May Queen chosen by vote – Ellen Earle.'

May 15th 1884 (G)
'A whole holiday granted by the managers in honour of Major Heathcote's Wedding with Miss Vachell.'

April 13th 1888 (I)
'A half holiday was given on Friday as a confirmation was held in the morning.'

February 8th 1889 (I)
'School closed at 3.30 as all the school children met at the Boys' School to see a Magic Lantern.'

A Magic Lantern was a popular form of Victorian entertainment. It was a forerunner of the slide projector, in which glass slides told stories or showed views, sometimes in colour. It was possible to give the illusion that the characters were moving, rather like a cartoon today.

September 19th 1890 (I)
'A half holiday was given as Hursley Guild went to Farley Mount for their annual outing.'

July 6th 1893 (I)
'A half holiday in honour of the marriage of the Duke of York with Princess May.'

May 1st 1896 (I)
'A whole holiday, being May Day. Owing to the illness of so many children, (measles) there was no May Queen this year.'

June 22nd 1897 (I)
'A whole holiday, the Queen's Diamond Jubilee. A fete in the Park to commemorate it.'

May 2nd 1898 (I)
'A whole holiday was given for the children to go 'Maying'. Emma Hicks was the Queen.'

The May Day custom of gathering spring flowers to decorate hoops to make into garlands was known as 'Maying.' The children paraded their garlands around the village, collecting pennies along the way. The money was used to fund a tea party for their parents.

The children elected the May Queen and she sat on a flower decked 'throne'. The girls wore white dresses and the boys wore their 'Sunday best.' They processed up to Park House on wagons and the May Queen was presented with more flowers. Maypole dancing, singing May Day songs and a tea were all part of the fun.

January 7th 1899 (I)
'The children had their New Year's Treat. Tea in the Girls' School at 3.30 after which each child received a present. At 5 o'clock they went to the Boys' School and were entertained by a conjuror.

The presents were –
- First Class boys: large drawing slates
- Second Class boys: tops
- Third Class boys: small drawing slates
- First Class girls: dolls
- Second and Third class girls: tea sets.'

October 15th 1899 (B)
'The school was assembled at 1 o'clock to be dismissed shortly after 3 o'clock on account of the opening of the new Workhouse.'

The Hursley Union workhouse was now too small. It held thirty-three inmates at the 1881 census. However, in 1894 Chandler's Ford was included in the 'catchment area' and larger premises were needed. The new workhouse was built using local bricks from the Chandler's Ford brickworks. It housed sixty residents to start with but there was plenty of room for extensions, when necessary. The building closed as a workhouse in 1925 and became 'Leigh House Hospital', a sanatorium for tuberculosis patients. In recent times it was demolished and the site used for private housing.

April 4th 1900 (G)
'In the afternoon the teachers and children walked nearly to Chandler's Ford to see the new Union.'

May 1st 1900 (G)
'A holiday for May garlanding. Emily Jones was chosen Queen of May.'

May 28th 1900 (G)
'The vicar brought a piece of smoked glass for the children to see the eclipse of the sun this afternoon. They went out in groups of 3 and saw it very well indeed.'

November 6th 1900 (B)
'School dismissed at 10.45 on account of the consecration of the new cemetery.'

The new cemetery was an extension to the churchyard graves area, a short walk away, at the top of Collins Lane. It is still the village cemetery.

February 5th 1901 (G)
'School closed on account of a deep snow and driving wind.'

May 1st 1901 (G)
'Dorothy Savage was elected Queen by ballot.'

May 3rd 1901 (G)
'A general lesson was given on the new well that has been made in the village.'

July 22nd 1901 (G)
'School finished at 12.30 in order to allow the children to attend the funeral service at 3 o'clock of the Dowager Lady Heathcote, a great benefactor to the school.'

June 26th 1902 (G)
'Attendance very thin today, this being the day fixed for the Coronation of King Edward and Queen Alexandra. This was to have been a holiday but the sad news of the King's serious illness and deferred Coronation made it seem right to postpone holidays.'

November 3rd 1902 (G)
'Play time extended for 10 minutes to allow the children to see the first meet of the Hursley Hounds which took place in the Vicar's meadow close to the playground.'

November 3rd 1902 (B)
'The boys were allowed to see the first meet of the hounds this morning.'

June 4th 1903 (G)
'The little daughter of Mr and Mrs Cooper, the new owners of the estate, wished to give a tea party to the children of the parish on this, her birthday, which was carried out.'

May 20th 1904 (B)
'Mrs Pinnick kindly gave the boys an entertainment on the gramophone during the last lesson.'

The Hursley Hunt was established in 1836.

Some of the fathers of Hursley 'scholars'.

July 27th 1905 (G)
'A Holiday – village cottage garden Flower Show.'

January 8th 1906 (G)
'This afternoon the school and children were photographed.'

April 9th 1907 (N)
'The Union Jack was hoisted today. Several boys heard the cuckoo. I heard it myself early this morning.'

May 8th 1907 (N)
'Annual tea to parents who are invited by the children. Expenses defrayed by the children themselves out of their May Day collecting boxes.'

May 24th 1907 (N)
'Distributed medals, shields and certificates for regular attendance.
Mary Vealey received a Bar in her medal for two years perfect attendance.'

Medals were awarded for excellent attendance and a 'bar' was added to indicate the number of years of 'excellence' for which the medal was given.

May 24th 1909 (N)
'Patriotic songs were sung, the meaning of Empire Day was explained and lessons on our duty as citizens of this great empire, lessons on our heritage, our privileges and the noble traits of kingly men were given.'

July 15th 1912 (N)
'King's visit to Winchester. Holiday.'

King George the Fifth and Queen Mary came to Winchester for a service of thanksgiving for the saving of Winchester cathedral by William Walker. William was a deep-water diver, who successfully shored up the foundations of the cathedral, after many months of working in darkness, water and wet peat. The king presented him with a silver rose bowl. Later he was awarded the M.V.O medal (Member of the Royal Victorian Order), for 'distinguished personal service to the monarch'.

September 18th 1918 (N)
'School closed each day in the afternoon for gathering blackberries. Weight 65 lb and 112 lb respectively.'

September 24th and October 1st 1918 (N)
'School closed for gathering blackberries.'

This gentle, carefree pursuit was taking place as the Great War was drawing to a close.

July 21st 1919 (N)
'Entertainment consisting of Morris Dancing, vocal drill and solo singing was given on Saturday on the lawn at Hursley Park in connection with the Peace Celebrations.'

January 24th 1921 (N)
'Took seventy-four children to the pantomime at Southampton today. We rode in motorbuses. All expenses were generously defrayed by Lady Cooper.'

February 28th 1922 (N)
'Princess Mary's wedding day. School closed.'

Princess Mary (the Princess Royal) was the only daughter of King Edward the Fifth and Queen Mary. She married Viscount Lascelles in Westminster Abbey.

November 7th 1923 (N)
'School closed for HRH Prince of Wales visit to Winchester.'

The next extract refers to Empire day, which was celebrated every year on Queen Victoria's birthday, May 24th. It was first celebrated, one year after Victoria died, in 1902, but was only officially recognised as an annual event in schools throughout the Empire, from 1916.

The aim of the day was to remind children that they were part of a wider British Empire and should feel proud of their country. The countries of the Empire were traditionally coloured pink or red on school world maps.

By the 1950's the Empire was declining as countries gained their independence and the day was re-named British Commonwealth Day. Queen Elizabeth II continued the tradition by sending a radio message to the young people of the Commonwealth countries on her official birthday, June 10th.

May 24th 1924 (N)
'Empire Day.
Schoolchildren, Boy Scouts and Girl Guides assembled in the school playground, a tableau of Britannia and the Empire arranged on a farm wagon, procession through the

village, headed by British Legion Band (Chandler's Ford) to Hursley Park. Sang 'Land of Hope and Glory', 'Rule Britannia' and 'God Save the King'. Tea and sports kindly provided by Sir George and Lady Cooper.'

September 8th 1924 (N)
'School reopened. Prizes at Hursley Flower Show –
Needlework – camisoles, pinafores, scarves, socks, drawing.
School gardening – potatoes, broad beans, peas, dwarf beans, carrots, turnips, beet, lettuce, from combined plots.'

Saturday May 23rd 1925 (N)
Empire Day
'School children assembled in playground and marched through the village, led by scout band, to the Park House. After an address by Sir Henry Burstal, the song 'Flag of Britain' was sung and the flag saluted by Scouts, Guides and children. During the evening by kind invitation of Sir George and Lady Cooper the children saw the film 'Zeebrugge'. The singing of 'Land of Hope and Glory' and the National Anthem by the entire audience concluded the celebration.'

The film 'Zeebrugge' depicted a daring raid by the Royal Navy and Royal Marines in 1918. They attempted to block the Zeebrugge canal in Belgium so that German U-boats and submarines could not come through to the English Channel from their base in Bruges, to endanger allied shipping. The raid failed but nevertheless involved much bravery for which medals were awarded.

December 15th 1925 (N)
'Children from Standards 3 to 7 gave a performance at the Working Men's Club this evening – Songs of the Winchester Festival. 28/9d was collected in aid of the Sports and Library Fund.'

December 16th 1925 (N)
'T.W. Ashton Esq. (Sir George Cooper's land agent) visited the school and arrangements were completed for the whole school to attend the Entertainment Hall, Hursley Park, on Sat. Dec. 19th to see a Christmas tree, given by Lady Cooper.'

Alan Rodbourne, a scholar at Hursley School at this time, remembers
enjoying the Christmas teas –
'We used to go across to the mansion for Christmas parties, all the children of the estate

workers. They used to come round with a wagon to pick us up. We went into the entertainment hall with a big Christmas tree, and a present.'

October 29th 1926 (N)
'An Exhibition of school was held this afternoon between 3 and 4 p.m. There being about forty parents present.'

March 9th 1927 (N)
'Twelve boys in Standards VI and VII visited the Hampshire County Council Farriery School in the village.'

This was a 'mobile blacksmith's shop' used for training purposes.

May 1st 1929 (JK)
'May Day celebration. Coronation of the first (newly opened) school May Queen with folk songs and dances. This was held in the Entertainment Hall (on the estate) and was followed by a haywain procession round the village with dancing in selected places. Buns and oranges, kindly provided by Lady Cooper, were distributed.'

The village forge in 1908.

The May Day haywain arrives outside Park House.

Lady Cooper presents the May Queen with flowers.

May 9th 1930 (JK)
'Headmaster (Mr Toyer) took whole of Class 1 and 2 boys 1¼ miles towards Otterbourne along King's Lane to see an excavator at work.'

King's Lane is now called Poles Lane.

June 7th 1932 (JK)
'School closed. All senior children, eighty-three in number, taken to Aldershot Tattoo Daylight Rehearsal. All expenses generously borne by Captain G. Cooper.'

October 8th 1934 (JK)
'Classes 1 and 2 taken up to the Park to see the banana tree fruiting in the hot houses.'

November 29th 1934 (JK)
'School closed – wedding of Prince George and Princess Marina of Greece.'

May 6th 1935 (JK)
'School closed for Jubilee Celebrations. Jubilee pageant for whole school.'

March 27th 1936 (JK)
'School closed at one day's notice in order that the children might witness the arrival of the 'Queen Mary' at Southampton. Made possible by the generous offer of Captain G. Cooper to defray expenses.'

The liner 'Queen Mary' sailed from Southampton on her maiden voyage to New York on May 27th, 1936.

May 11th 1937 (JK)
''School closed for Coronation and Whitsun.'

May 14th 1937 (JK)
'Thirty-two senior children taken to London during the Whitsun holiday to see Buckingham Palace, Trafalgar Square, Whitehall, Downing Street, Westminster, Houses of Parliament, Thames Embankment, St Paul's, Piccadilly, Regent Street, Oxford Street and 3 trips on the underground.'

September 28th 1945 (JK)
'School closed for agricultural potato picking holiday – to reopen October 15th.'

October 4th 1946 (JK)
'School closed for fortnight potato picking holiday.'

May 19th 1947 (JK)
'School photographs taken during break in afternoon.'

September 24th 1947 (JK)
'Mobile cinema films shown at 2 p.m. today. Chief film was 'Beginnings of History'. It was particularly instructive. Another was 'Lumbering in Canada' but the children's choice as the best was 'Birds of the Countryside'.'

June 3rd 1948 (JK)
'Twenty-four senior boys taken to see the Hampshire v. Australia cricket match at Southampton.'

The Australians were all out for 117 in the first innings and the match was abandoned due to a hailstorm.

July 19th 1948 (JK)
'Arrangements made for parties to go to Bull Drove baths in Romsey. Nineteen went today.'

December 17th 1948 (JK)
'In the afternoon an entertainment began at 2p.m. consisting of a conjuror, tea and ice creams kindly provided by Lady Cooper.'

Cicely Bull remembers Christmas fun in the 1950's –

'We had a conjuror who came in, Professor Woodley. We had a tea – well, it was probably a sandwich and a cake – that Sir George and Lady Cooper would provide. My mum couldn't help because she had a child at the school and she might give me an extra cake or something. Anybody with children there wasn't allowed to help.'

July 27th 1950 (JK)
'Captain Sir George Cooper Bart generously gave a whole day's summer treat by sending all except the 'babies' to Regents Park Zoo.'

September 18ᵗʰ 1950 (JK)
'On Saturday an exhibition of all types of work done by each class was staged at a fete in the village: craft, art and rural studies.'

July 27ᵗʰ 1951 (JK)
'The school was open from 2.15 to 7.30 today to enable parents, friends and managers to see the work. All work done or being done during the term was shown from the babies' first efforts to the seniors. Manuscript work and exercise books were open to inspection. The rooms were crowded from start to finish. The experiment proved a great success.'

October 12ᵗʰ 1951 (JK)
'School closed owing to army manoeuvres.'

The Royal Artillery was on its way to Southampton to join the United Nations Forces, supporting South Korea in the Korean War.

May 26ᵗʰ 1955 (JK)
'School closed today as it is to be used as a Polling Station for the General election.'

Peter Smithers was elected as the Conservative member for Winchester.

May 5ᵗʰ 1959 (JK)
'Class 1 went by coach to Romsey baths this afternoon for first swimming lesson.'

May 7ᵗʰ 1959 (JK)
'School closed. Class 1, twenty two children, accompanied by myself, Miss Sloan, Mrs Shorto, Mrs Richards and Mrs Welch, visited London Museums.'

June 10ᵗʰ 1959 (JK)
'Top class taken to Romsey for rounders matches with Romsey County Primary School.'

May 6ᵗʰ 1960 (JK)
'School holiday for Princess Margaret's wedding.'

July 21ˢᵗ 1961 (JK)
'We held a Bring and Buy sale for the children only. £11 5s was raised and has gone to augment the gift from the Hursley flower show committee for the television.'

July 24th 1963 (JK)

'This afternoon we held our Open day. About 150 came. They were entertained by singing, acting, etc. by each class. Parents wandered in to see children's books. At 3.15, Mr Wilkie Cooper presented Mrs Shorto with a cheque on her retirement.'

14

Drums, horses and troops

FEW communities in England remained untouched by the Great War. The noise and spectacle of troop movements disturbed the peace of Hursley and its school. Loss of life was felt too. The war memorial in the village records the names of all who volunteered to fight in the Great War, not simply those who died. Only thirty-four men failed to return to Hursley at the end of the conflict.

There is also a Commemoration Seat, erected by Sir George Cooper, under the tree facing the main road, near John Keble School. This has the names of all the British Army Units in the Eighth Division who assembled in tents in the Park in October 1914. Between ten and twenty thousand men marched the 8 miles to Southampton at noon on November 4th, ready to embark for Le Havre on November 14th, to fight on the Western Front.

October 26th 1914 (N)
'The movement of troops hinders the work.'

October 29th 1914 (N)
'March out of the troops. The school was closed this afternoon.'

December 23rd 1914 (N)
'The coming and departure of troops, the noises of drums, bugles, horses, men, gun carriages, tractor engines and an unsettled staff has made the work very trying and difficult.'

March 19th 1917 (N)
'Leonard Roud was sent for during the dinner hour. News has just arrived that his brother is killed in France.'

October 22nd 1917 (N)
'Two of our old children living in London have come to stay in Hursley during the air raids.'

Thirty-four Hursley men failed to return from the Great War.

Two members of the 'Roud' family are mentioned as volunteers on the war memorial. Only one returned.

April 26th 1918 (N)
'Sir George Cooper Bart has presented the school with a large map of the War Area of the Western Front.'

September 16th 1918 (N)
'James Elder, an old scholarship boy and Lt. in the Flying Corps killed in France. Body and machine found in the advance.'

The Royal Flying Corps had eighty-four aircraft in service in 1914.

September 20th 1918 (N)
'Percy Grills truanting. Has been sleeping with the soldiers in the camp.'

Sir George Cooper, who bought the estate in 1902, and was made a baronet in 1905, was married to a wealthy American heiress. She funded a United States Military Hospital in the Park in 1917, housing four hundred and fifty patients in wooden buildings. It was demolished at the end of 1918. She also gave over the upper floor of Park House to be used as a hospital for up to fifty officers, which she paid for.

James Elder's name on the war memorial.

Sir George gave an amazing 5 million pounds towards the war effort, the largest known private donation for this purpose.

November 11th 1927 (JK)
'Armistice Day observed. Address given by Master and two minutes silence. Names of old boys who have paid the supreme sacrifice was read out during the salute.'

15

Air raids, evacuees and gas masks

THE Second World War brought changes to the village and its school. In 1940 bombing raids at the Vickers Supermarine premises in Southampton led to the Spitfire design offices being moved into Park House. Here they stayed until 1956. A hanger for testing aircraft engines was built next to the school and the noise from this was very disruptive to school work.

Evacuees arriving from Southampton increased the class numbers and school routine was interrupted with blackouts being arranged for the rooms. Dances for the troops were provided at the school.

Alan Rodbourne tells us about his school wartime memories:

'We had baffle walls that went all round the school and the windows were moved so if anything happened you could get out and they'd protect the glass from getting blown in. There weren't any air raid shelters in the village.

We had a couple of army wives stopping with us; they were always there in the evenings. Dad was in the Home Guard so he was off in the evenings. Their HQ was in the cellar of the King's Head and they used to patrol, standing up in the cemetery, just like Dad's Army.'

September 4th 1939 (JK)
'School closed. War declared on Germany on Sunday September 3rd.'

September 7th 1939 (JK)
'HMI called to enquire about the number of evacuated children of school age from Southampton. School used as a distribution centre for whole district for rations and personnel.'

September 25th 1939 (JK)
'24 evacuees admitted.'

Hursley's own 'Dad's Army' – The Home Guard in front of the protected school walls.

These children would have come from Southampton, which was badly bombed.

November 27th 1939 (JK)
'From today, afternoon session ends at 3.30 in order that children having long distances to walk may reach home before the blackout time.'

January 8th 1940 (JK)
'Miss Mason, an evacuated teacher from Basset Green Infants, (Southampton) reported for duty.'

April 25th 1940 (JK)
'All paths and flowers and half the boys' individual plots are to be used for cropping vegetables for the period of the war.'

May 27th 1940 (JK)
'School to be used for gathering station for refugees.'

May 28th 1940 (JK)
'Correspondent decided to use passage and part of lobby for ARP (Air Raid Precaution) shelter – wood to be sent from estate. Windows to be painted with 'Splinter Proof' and all glass in passage and lobby to be covered with boarded screens or stiff fabric of some kind.'

June 4th 1940 (JK)
'Daily practice and ARP (Air Raid Precaution) drill has been taken every day. Two cupboards for rations for refugees have been prepared.
Staff room to be utilised for emergency first-aid in case of air raids but will also have windows seen to.
Daily practice by senior boys in use of stirrup pumps for fire services.'

June 11th 1940 (JK)
'Letter received from LEA (Local Education Authority) refusing to buy 4 sheets of hardboard to make the school passage an ARP refuge. Work done by headmaster and senior boys during last fortnight is therefore nullified and time wasted.
Senior boys set to work to render the windows safe by other means.'

July 3rd 1940 (JK)
'First daylight air raid warning 9.10 a.m. Ceased at 9.45 a.m. Children filed into passage as practised.'

July 16th 1940 (JK)
'Miss Cutsforth returned to duty. Reason for absence – had been within twenty-two yards of bombs falling during night of 14th.'

November 11th 1940 (JK)
'Number of evacuees risen to forty one.'

February 4th 1941 (JK)
'ARP Warden inspected the children's gas marks.'

July 21st 1941 (JK)
'School in occupation of the army for the weekend.'

January 5th 1942 (JK)
'Workmen in Class 1 and 2 rooms scraping windows and applying fresh netting against bomb splinters.'

February 20th 1942 (JK)
'WRDC (Winchester Rural District Council) delivered 126 blankets and 12 camp beds today for Panic Evacuation Rest Centre at this school.'

June 22nd 1942 (JK)
'Sharp air raid last night. Only 70 present this morning. Workmen doing the 'blackout' during morning.'

November 3rd 1942 (JK)
'School used by army for dance during holiday – left without rearranging. Children and teachers sent home.'

Many overseas allies were camped at varying times with the British Forces in the Park and would have been glad of some nighttime entertainment.

November 5th 1942 (JK)
'School could not commence until 9.25 as blackout not fully taken down and desks in disorder after Home Guard parade of night before.'

November 16th 1942 (JK)
'School could not commence until 9.40 owing to a Saturday night's dance for the KOSB

(Kings Own Scottish Borderers) stationed here. Head teacher and 4 boys clearing and sweeping until 9.35. Broken glass together with all the dance sweepings of the whole of school had been thrown onto the asphalt playground at front of school.'

June 1st 1943 (JK)
'All children were to go through gas chamber today but it was only possible to put eighty through in the time. Remainder will go through at some future time.'

To make sure the children's gas masks were functioning properly, a lorry arrived at school, with a container. The children walked through a corridor in this container, wearing their masks, while tear gas was pumped through. If their eyes were streaming at the end, they were given new gas masks to replace the faulty ones.

April 3rd 1945 (JK)
'Mrs Buck's husband is home on leave from N. Africa after 3½ years. She has agreed to work in the mornings but wishes the afternoons free.'

May 8th 1945 (JK)
'Germany accepted unconditional surrender – two days holiday declared.'

May 23rd 1945 (JK)
'An old scholar of the school Reginald Richards, Royal marines, 4 years prisoner of war, came in and gave a talk to the children on his experience.'

Eight Hursley men died in service in World War Two.

16

Swearing, falsehoods and cruelty
to a goat

PUNISHMENTS were carefully recorded in the logbooks. Interestingly, even girls were given 'a stripe' (a stroke on the hand with the cane) for misdemeanours.

January 20th 1864 (G)
'Had occasion to reprove the Second Class for rudeness and keep them for half an hour after school to learn a lesson as a punishment.'

February 16th 1864 (G)
'Five girls were kept to write lessons on their slates after school hours.'

April 11th 1864 (G)
'Three girls kept after school to finish some needlework which had been badly done and consequently taken out.'

May 6th 1864 (G)
'Kept a class after school for coming in from church in a disorderly manner.'

March 31st 1865 (G)
'I met with 1 case of obstinacy today with which I had some trouble in dealing. Kept the child for some time after school.'

October 29th 1866 (B)
'Great noise owing to two boys having mice in school.'

January 17th 1867 (G)
'The whole of the First Class kept back to write their psalms on their slates having been most imperfectly repeated to Mrs Young.'

Mrs Young was the wife of the vicar who succeeded Rev John Keble.

April 10th 1867 (G)
'Kept the whole school in for twenty minutes for coming in noisily from church.'

March 11th 1868 (B)
'Choir boys reprimanded, bad behaviour in church.'

March 12th 1868 (B)
'Window broken, game stopped that caused it.'

June 27th 1870 (B)
'Admonished several boys from Infants' School. Punished W. Wild for telling a falsehood.'

October 21st 1872 (B)
'Punished several boys for bringing chestnuts to school.'

November 20th 1872 (B)
'Punished James Beavis and Fred Streeter for fighting in the street during the dinner hour.'

January 28th 1873 (B)
'Fred Streeter played truant.'

July 7th 1874 (B)
'Punished James Beavis for making Henry Waterage's nose bleed.'

May 23rd 1879 (B)
'Mr Bailey, Sir William's head keeper, visited the school and complained of boys breaking the Park fence in endeavouring to take birds' nests.'

November 28th 1879 (B)
'Ernest Wild has been away for the last 3 days owing to a pain in his side caused by a fall which, it is supposed, he had, while having a chastisement for disobedience and attempting to throw a book at the master's head.'

May 6th 1881 (G)
'Three girls, Amelia Wild, Sophia Whitmarsh and Florence Clark sent to the vicar to be reproved for naughtiness. He desired that they might be kept apart in disgrace and not allowed to come to the May Feast.'

September 12th 1884 (B)
'Resumed school this week. Boys, as usual, have forgotten much of their work.'

September 19th 1884 (B)
'Much energy is wanted to get them to settle to their work.'

December 5th 1884 (B)
'The vicar called on Tuesday and gave boys a scolding for going into the holly hedge.'

June 29th 1892 (B)
'I had to chastise John Pack for swearing – this is the second time. I have given him 4 stripes.'

June 16th 1893 (B)
'I had to chastise Edwin Hall this morning for playing truant, giving him 3 stripes on the hand.'

January 23rd 1895 (B)
'As Greenaway is frequently late I have found it expedient to give him a stripe or two on the hand with the stick. He has been better in this respect since.'

February 22nd 1895 (B)
'Horace Shepherd was punished for using bad language in the playground.'

July 26th 1900 (GI)
'Punished Amelia Callan for disobedience – 1 stroke.'

January 20th 1905 (B)
"Had to punish some boys severely this morning for calling into the Girls' School and looking through the windows.'

May 21ˢᵗ 1906 (B)
'Many of the windows of the School Cottage were broken. The offenders were C. and P. Bunney and E. and A. Chiverton. These were punished.'

June 11ᵗʰ 1906 (B)
'Wm. Diaper and P. Bunney were punished for throwing stones. I caught them both in the act. I cautioned the whole school against this practice and climbing on walls.'

January 20ᵗʰ 1909 (N)
'W. Diaper and P. Bunney punished for breaking through fences near the school.'

These two seem to be often in trouble. See the entry above for June 1906.

No school today?

February 17th 1916 (N)
'A girl in Standard IV was punished – 1 stripe on each hand. This girl is wilfully disobedient to each teacher in charge and absolutely defiant. Other means of punishment have failed.'

July 21st 1919 (N)
'Punished a child for rude conduct.'

June 27th 1921 (N)
'A boy received 4 strokes on the hand for indecent conduct in the school.'

September 23rd 1921 (N)
'A boy (13) punished with 4 stripes for cruelty to a goat.'

October 3rd 1922 (N)
'Outbreak of swearing in the school. The children were punished.'

Alan Rodbourne remembers his punishments from Mr Toyer (headmaster) and Mrs Shorto, class teacher.

'There was 1 punishment that used to suit us fine. Mrs Shorto used to take piano lessons first thing in the morning and we used to hate it, so to upset her we used to start whistling. She used to say 'out' and we had to go and stand under the clock. Old Toyer had his office right opposite there and he used to come out and say, 'What've you been up to? Whistling again I suppose?'
We said we had and he'd say, 'Go on out in the garden out of the way and do some gardening.'

So of course we'd go off out in the garden and unless anybody told us to go back in that day, we stayed there! And when the bell used to go we used to dive in the old pigsty and stop there until someone missed us.

The worst time I got the cane was from Mrs Shorto and that was my fault. There must have been 1 of the nippers behind me playing about. She was walking around and she caught him playing about behind me and I heard 'bang'. I said, 'Missed!' But she never 'missed' the next time!

Mrs Shorto would send you down to the Infants' class to cool off and you'd have to go and sit down there and look a fool.

She wouldn't have no nonsense. If anyone swore or anything like that she'd grab hold of you by the scruff of the neck and you'd be out in the sink and she'd wash your mouth out with soap and water.

We used to go out and play football and we used to make out we never heard the bell and just stayed out there. Mr Toyer used to come across and get us in. Then he asked us, 'Did you hear the bell?' Some used to say 'no' and some used to say 'yes'. Those that said 'yes' got away with it but those that said they never heard it, they got a clout! If you 'owned up' you were all right!'

17

The mystery of Mrs Dickman's spectacles, police investigations and royalty

May 6ᵗʰ 1932 (JK)
'Miss Laidman absent from duty as called as witness in case of the attempted stealing of her car from school premises.'

January 21ˢᵗ 1936 (JK)
'Death of His Majesty George V.'

January 22ⁿᵈ 1936 (JK)
'The two Classes 1 and 2 listened to proclamation announcing new king, Edward VIII.'

January 28ᵗʰ 1936 (JK)
'School closed. Funeral of late king George V.'

March 1ˢᵗ 1940 (JK)
'Sir George A. Cooper Bart, chairman of the governors, died today. Funeral is to be on Monday.'

January 19ᵗʰ 1944 (JK)
'School Correspondent asked for a list of children with 1½ miles to walk to school who need rubber wellingtons.'

April 25ᵗʰ 1944 (JK)
'A father called re – his boy, convicted on March 29ᵗʰ for setting fire to an oat rick and binder and sent to a remand home for a month's observation. A report from the school was queried by the parent, particularly the term 'subnormal'. The teacher had used it to imply he was academically below the Standard of his class, not 'mentally subnormal'.

February 24th 1948 (JK)
'All glass from school garden 'lights' found taken at 7.30 a.m. Was seen intact last night. Police notified. This follows cutting of all children's spring cabbage during the holidays and all brussels sprouts during first week of term.'

February 7th 1952
'His Majesty the king, George VI, died in his sleep.'

July 1st 1953 (JK)
'School closed for two days on occasion of Coronation of Queen Elizabeth 2nd.'

June 4th 1954 (JK)
'This evening a whist drive was held in the village hall, Catways, in aid of the school wireless fund. £20 2s was realised.'

'Catways' was a very basic village hall known as the Hut.

July 30th 1954 (JK)
'School timetable disorganised slightly this afternoon so that children could observe the eclipse of the sun.'

March 14th 1956 (JK)
'Sir George Cooper presented the school with a beautifully framed picture of the Queen.'

November 26th 1956 (JK)
'It was noticed that during the weekend the flat roofs on either side of the building had been stripped of lead. It was reported to the local constable who came to inspect the damage and question about the matter.'

December 19th 1956 (JK)
'£2 17s sent off for sale of Spastic stamps.'

The term 'spastic' was used in the 1950's without any fear of causing offence.

January 20th 1958 (JK)
'Mrs Smith noticed this morning that another sheet of lead has been taken from the roof during the weekend. PC Abbott came to inspect the damage.'

July 14th 1960 (JK)
'Mr Peter Maggs and Mr Ron Carey from the BBC came during the dinner hour to make some recordings which will be used in a programme on Aug 12th at 6.35 p.m.'

July 22nd 1960 (JK)
'This afternoon we held our annual Bring and Buy Sale. We raised £12 10s, our highest total yet.'

January 10th 1961 (JK)
'I attended the funeral of Sir George Cooper Bart, Chairman of the managers.
A wreath was subscribed for by all the staff and children. He has been a great friend to the school and will be sadly missed.'

June 9th 1961 (JK)
'During the night the school has been broken into and 3 cupboards forced. 19s 6d dinner money stolen, 7s 6d needlework money, 4s phone and £5 of savings stamps. PC Hodaway and members of CID investigated.'

September 22nd 1961 (JK)
'During the night someone had forced entry into the staff room and forced open cupboards. Nothing taken.'

December 18th 1961 (JK)
'School broken into during the weekend. Small sum missing from phone box.'

March 2nd 1962 (JK)
'During last evening the staff room was entered by breaking a window. The record player was stolen.'

January 31st 1963 (JK)
'Disruption of work this afternoon because during the dinnertime a child took Mrs Dickman's spectacles in the case. Despite all questioning, at this stage, culprit not known.'

Mrs Dickman was the younger children's class teacher.

February 1st 1963 (JK)
'Mrs Smith (caretaker) persuaded the culprit to admit her guilt and to find the spectacles behind the toilets.'

March 4th 1963 (JK)
'Mr Peter Maggs, a BBC radio reporter, came and talked with some children from Class 1. A recording was made.'

December 6th 1963 (JK)
'This evening Mr Peter Maggs came to talk to some of Class 1 and some scholars who have recently left for secondary school. A recording was made. The subject was the death of President Kennedy.'

The inscription on the bell reads:
'This bell was given to the school in memory of Dorothy 'Dotty' Dickman, a teacher at the school for forty years, by Duncan McDonald, a former resident, who is very grateful for the help she gave him. (September 1995)'

18

Miss Lily Flower, Mr Whippe and Mrs Warr

INTRODUCING the staff, pupil teachers and monitors.

'Pupil teachers', who had to be at least 13 years old, helped the teacher, often taking lessons by themselves. They followed a paid 5-year apprenticeship to become a certificated teacher. They often came into school an hour early to receive training from the head teacher and sometimes the training took place on a Saturday. Pupil teachers are not mentioned in the logbooks after 1885.

Older, reliable and able pupils were sometimes used to hep as 'monitors', when the teacher was overwhelmed by large numbers or unable to attend. Monitors could be as young as 12 and were often given heavy responsibilities

Miss Lucy Lampet was Mistress of the Girls' School for 44 years, from 1862 until her retirement in 1906. However, there were frequent changes of Master in the Boys' School and this fact was noted in various Inspectors' reports as being unsettling for the scholars.

Before the Second World War, women teachers were expected to resign if they got married, hence they were traditionally referred to as 'Miss'.

This is a list of the headmasters, headmistresses and assistant teachers.

1866 – 68 Henry Plumridge
1868 – 70 Henry Cooper
1870 – 74 Sam Waite
1875 – 76 Windsor Vokes
1876 – 77 Charles Shuttleworth
1878 – September to December – Thomas Pickering
1878 – 1888 John Jennings
1888 – 1892 A.J. Hughes
1892 – 1922 William Orchard

1922 – 1928 David Cleary
1928 – September till November – Mr Whippe
1928 – 1953 Mr Toyer
1953 – 1976 Mrs Warr

November 8th 1863 (G)
'Pupil teacher absent. Her class taken by the oldest first class girl, Isabella Stanford.'

September 3rd 1866 (B)
'Henry Plumridge, Schoolmaster, with 1 monitor, opened school with 33 scholars.'

January 28th 1867 (G)
'School taken charge of by the pupil teacher, kindly assisted by Mrs Young in the absence of the Schoolmistress through illness.'

February 26th 1867 (G)
'Used 2 First Class girls as monitors, 1 for a few who do not know their letters.'

March 19th 1867 (B)
'Employed John Heath as regular monitor.'

October 2nd 1868 (B)
'Resigned the charge of this school having accepted a situation as organist in Oxford.'
(Henry Plumridge.)

October 12th 1868 (B)
'Henry Cooper, Schoolmaster, took charge.'

April 22nd 1869 (B)
'Heard pupil teacher teach his class.'

May 19th 1869 (G)
'A very wet day, consequently a very thin attendance indeed. Infant School taught by a monitor.'

May 23rd 1870 (B)
'New Schoolmaster Mr Sam Waite.'

March 1871 (B)
Inspector's Report

'The school has suffered in numbers and efficiency by change of teacher.'

December 24th 1874 (B)
'Resigned the charge of this school.'

January 25th 1875 (B)
'New Schoolmaster Windsor Vokes
Children rough and disorderly from the long holidays.'

April 19th 1876 (B)
'Wm. Hicks, pupil teacher, sent away for obstinate disobedience to the Master in school. The said pupil teacher receives his lessons at the Master's House at 7 a.m. On Thursday he came late at 7.13 a.m. As he has been wilfully remissable with his lessons I sent him home again. He came to school at 9 but let his class go on anyhow and was snappish with the boys. In the afternoon I requested him to question his class on the lesson they had just read. This he obstinately would not do. I sent him home. I saw his parents in the evening who were exceedingly sorry that he had been so bad. I leniently promised to give him another trial. He came the next day but was as sulky as ever. On Saturday he spoke most impertinently to me in the street. I wrote to the Rev Young, one of the managers, requesting his removal. I likewise told his friends that he was not to come to school again till the managers' decision.'

August 3rd 1876 (B)
'Master resigned.'

New Schoolmaster in December – Charles Shuttleworth.

December 20th 1876 (B)
'Found the school backward in dictation and much in need of firm discipline. Very little geography and history is known throughout the school.'

April 27th 1877 (G)
'Lesson given by pupil teacher to the gallery of collected classes on The Manufacture of Glass.'

January 3rd 1878 (B)
'John Jennings – Schoolmaster.'

April 22nd 1878 (B)
'W. Hicks has been removed from the register of pupil teachers serving in this school.'

September 10th 1878 (B)
'Thomas Pickering in charge.'

Mr Pickering left at the end of December that year.

October 4th 1878 (G)
'Pupil teacher's oral lesson on The Volcanoes of South America.
Emily Parker, a candidate for the office of pupil teacher began working in the Infants'
School this week.'

January 6th 1880 (G)
'Fanny Hanks, a candidate for the office of pupil teacher, began her work in school today working with Alethea C. Edgington who is leaving us in a week for the Training College in Salisbury, after an apprenticeship of 5 years. She obtained a first class scholarship.'

December 23rd 1880 (I)
'Duties resigned by Miss Colson on her marriage. Miss Diaper to take charge.'

May 27th 1881 (I)
'Duties resigned by Miss Doris Diaper in consequence of a notice from the Council Office that she was not qualified as a provisionally certificated teacher.'

December 21st 1883 (I)
'Isabel Laidlaw resigned the charge of the school through ill health.'

January 7th 1885 (I)
'Catherine Mackay provisionally certificated teacher, formerly a pupil teacher at Orpington, Kent, entered upon the duties of this school as senior assistant to the Girls' Mistress.'

November 25th 1887 (I)
'Fanny Earle, a Standard VII girl, has taken charge of the Infants during the absence of the mistress.'

May 25th 1888 (I)
'Resigned my duties as mistress of this school. Catherine Mackay.'

July 6th 1888 (B)
'Resigned charge of this school. John F. Jennings'

July 16th 1888 (B)
'A.J. Hughes commenced duties as Master.'

May 20th 1904 (B)
'Staff – William Orchard and Miss J. Kingsgate.'

December 12th 1907 (N)
'Miss Coleman, a teacher on 'Supply', came to give temporary assistance in place of Miss Westbrook who is ill.'

This is the first reference in the logbooks to the 'Supply Teacher System' of replacing an absent teacher with a temporary one.

March 1st 1915 (N)
'Miss Lampet buried. Since Miss North left on July 31st last year we have had supply teachers on and off. I am single handed again in the main room. It is impossible to make satisfactory progress.'

June 1st 1915 (N)
'Miss Sinclair commenced teaching in the Infants' room.'

July 21st 1915 (N)
'Miss Sinclair not well. The journey to and from Winchester is really too much. She walks both ways.'

It's difficult to imagine a teacher walking 5 miles to school and back today.

February 18th 1919 (N)
'I am left without a single member of staff (illness).'

HMI report December 1919 (N)
'The Master (Mr Orchard) has been essaying the impossible task of teaching 83 scholars in 6 grades of work. This unsettled state has lasted from Nov 1917 with various resignations and absences due to illness.

The Master has done all that lay in his power in a most unsparing way with the net result, so far as he is concerned, that breakdown appeared to be inevitable in consequence of the nervous and physical strains involved. Urgent representations were made by the managers to the LEA in the hope of getting immediate relief. Some temporary help was given but there still appears to be a vacancy in the third class.'

Mr Orchard continued his onerous task for two and a half more years, despite the stress and strain of very large class numbers.

May 1st 1922 (N)
'I, David Arthur Cleary, this day took over the duties of Headmaster.'

June 16th 1922 (N)
'The headmaster (William Orchard) retires after 16 years service.'

March 2nd 1925 (N)
'Miss Eva Margaret Harris (age 20) commenced work today in charge of Class 4, (Infants and Standard 1)'

March 11th 1925 (N)
'Miss Tuffield absent. She received news that her fiancé was killed in an accident on the Southampton Road last night.'

March 12th 1925 (N)
'Miss Tuffield absent attending the inquest.'

March 13th 1925 (N)
'Miss Tuffield absent attending the funeral.'

Staff List March 1925 (N)
'David Cleary – Head master,
Edith Tuffield,
Miss Bray,
Eva Margaret Harris'

September 10th 1925 (N)
'Miss Tuffield taken ill in school.'

October 12th 1925 (N)
'Received news this morning that Miss Tuffield died on Saturday in Winchester hospital. The vicar visited the school and took prayers.'

November 23rd 1925 (N)
'Miss Laidman (age 28) commenced work and is taking Class 3 – Standards IV and V.'

July 26th 1926 (N)
'Death of G. Taylor – caretaker.'

February 7th 1927 (N)
'Mrs Eades caretaker.'

June 25th 1928 (N)
'Today received appointment as headmaster of Denmead Council School and gave 3 months notice. David A. Cleary'

September 3rd 1928 (JK)
'I take charge of the school this morning. M. F. Whippe'

November 30th 1928 (JK)
'I terminate my duties today.'

No further explanation is given for such a short-term appointment.

December 3rd 1928 (JK)
'I, Arthur M. Toyer, commenced my duties as headmaster.'

September 9th 1929 (JK)
'Miss Bray tendered her resignation in view of her approaching marriage in October.'

May 6th 1930 (JK)
'Mrs Dorothy Dickman reported for duty this morning.'

The Schoolhouse in the 1920s. Perhaps the gentleman in the picture is Mr Toyer.

October 16th 1945 (JK)
'Report of HMI.
The headmaster has been here some 16 years. No boy or girl can fail to benefit who passes through his hands. He has made this school a model of the best type of the old country 'All Standard School.' '

September 28th 1946 (JK)
'Miss Anne Sloan commenced duties.'

February 8th 1949 (JK)
'Mrs Shorto absent. She is now under the doctor.'

June 13th 1949 (JK)
'It appears likely that for the first time since February the full complement of teachers will be on duty.'

June 14th 1949 (JK)
'Sir George Cooper spoke to the assembled school about the honour done to the school by the award of the MBE conferred on the Headmaster.'

This award was in recognition of Mr Toyer's services to rural education.

January 4th 1950 (JK)
'Mrs Shorto and 2 senior children released from 2 p.m. to 3.10 p.m. in order to take wreaths to the funeral of Mrs Dickman's husband.'

March 26th 1953 (JK)
'Mrs Warr, newly appointed head teacher, paid a visit to look over the school. Present head retiring next week.'

September 24th 1953 (JK)
'We heard the sad news that Mr Toyer MBE, the late headmaster, has died suddenly. We shall miss his visits very much.'

October 1st 1953 (JK)
'The vicar took assembly this morning as a short memorial service to Mr Toyer. A collection has been made and will be sent to Dr Barnardo's Orphanage in tribute to his memory.'

October 9th 1953 (PS)
'HMI Report.
This school was reorganised as a Primary School in January when thirty-five of the oldest pupils transferred to the Secondary Modern Schools in Winchester.
There are now 139 children, organised in 4 classes.
Some words deserve to be said regarding that quarter of a century of the school's history, which closed with the former headmaster's retirement in April. He was appointed in 1928 and at the age of 72 years was causing his charges to enjoy the skill and wisdom of a teaching lifetime of 47 years.
He was a headmaster richly gifted to deal with children of all ages and especially with country children. His original and beneficent mind threw up innovations which continuously refreshed the teaching of the whole school.'

June 20th 1955 (PS)
'This weekend our caretaker Mr Smith has died. Mrs Smith is continuing to do the work temporarily.'

July 1st 1963 (PS)
'Mr Littlecroft called to present Mrs Shorto with a 'Golden Letter' in appreciation, on her retirement, of her many years service in this school.'

19

Empire, 'wands' for drill and our English kings

HISTORY and geography were part of the curriculum but in the early years lessons relied mainly on the pupils reading about past events and other countries, with, it appears, little input from the teacher.

Further explanation of 'drill' (P.E.) can be found in chapter 7.

December 16th 1863 (G)
'Miss Simeon gave a lesson on the Geography of England and Wales to the First Class.'

February 28th 1866 (G)
'Gave a Geography lesson to the first class on the Chief Manufacturers of the United Kingdom. I am afraid they take little interest in lessons of this kind generally. Kept the late girls.'

October 5th 1877 (G)
'Nearly every child present.
Timetable strictly followed: Standard VI began learning decimals. In Geography 1st and 3rd classes had lessons together on Africa.'

February 6th 1880 (G)
'Geography course – have been going over the old ground again and this week have gone rapidly over North America.'

December 16th 1892 (B)
'First Class finished the Geography of America.'

October 18th 1895 (B)
'The Upper Division has now been through the Geography of the World and revised that of France, Holland and Spain.'

November 28th 1895 (B)
'Began the geography of Africa and gave lesson on management of poultry.'

February 27th 1903 (B)
'End of school year. Average attendance 32.
In the HMI Approved Scheme of Work for 1903 for History, Standard 3 are to read a history book.'

December 22nd 1903 (B)
'Received wands for drill.'

Scheme of work for 1907/8 (N)
'History – a 3-year course for upper Standards – on English kings. Each course will endeavour to show how our Empire has been built up – our constitutional heritage – and the noble deeds of great men and women.
For girls (if time and circumstances allow) Drawing, Shorthand and Health and Moral Training.'

20

Cuckoos, orchids and a pure white mole

FROM the early 1900's, far more effort is made to introduce the children to local natural history.

June 21ˢᵗ 1909 (N)
'Brought an unusually large specimen of a water beetle into school today and allowed all children to examine it.'

July 12ᵗʰ 1909 (N)
'Today I brought in a jay which was shot on Friday. We compared and contrasted it with our local birds.'

March 6ᵗʰ 1912 (N)
'The orchid 'dendrobrium nobile' was painted in Drawing today. The specimens came from Southend greenhouses. Some rare specimens of wild orchid are found in Hursley. The following orchid specimens have been brought to school for lessons – bee, butterfly, spotted sweet-scented, dwarf, bird's nest and broom-rape.'

July 12ᵗʰ 1912 (N)
'Last Thursday we had a dead cuckoo in school and oral lessons given. We had a fine specimen of an English snake – 30 inches long.'

April 19ᵗʰ 1917 (N)
'A class of twenty boys were taken to an uncultivated allotment to work on the Communal System.'

German U-boat blockades meant that rationing had to be introduced during the Great War. Any spare allotments were used to grow vegetables to provide extra food for the villagers.

April 26th 1917 (N)
'We have taken over another allotment for food production, planting mainly potatoes.'

September 16th 1918 (N)
'Harry Jones caught a sparrow hawk in his garden net. It was trying to kill a small chicken. He brought the bird to school, alive, and I exhibited it to each group of children.'

March 3rd 1925 (N)
'A pure white mole was brought to school by John Taylor. Nature lessons on the mole were taken.'

June 26th 1928 (JK)
'A thrush has built a nest in a small tree in the boys' playground and today was seen teaching 4 young to fly. A spotted fly catcher has built on the side of a tree in the path leading to the school, having today 4 eggs.'

July 17th 1928 (JK)
'Three nestlings left the nest today.'

May 7th 1929 (JK)
'Lady Cooper thanked those children who had brought primroses last Saturday for the London Hospitals.'

On Maunday Thursdays it was the tradition for the children to pick primroses in Ampfield Woods. Lady Cooper packed them up and sent them to Great Ormond Street Children's Hospital. She provided tea for the pickers.

November18th 1935 (JK)
'Dairy Classes begun this morning under County Dairy teacher. Class held in mornings this week in teachers' room. Fifteen boys attended, this being all the boys in the Senior Class. All are over 12 years.
Next week the classes will be held in the dairy or milking sheds of Home Farm, Hursley Park.'

Almost all the men in the village worked on the estate as farm labourers, gardeners, carpenters, plumbers, builders, butlers, cooks and grooms. Their sons would no doubt follow suit so long as work was available. It would have been in the estate's interests to show support for these relevant training classes.

The estate dairy.

21

Rats, a new school and the flooded stokehole

March 11th 1864 (G)
'Lady Heathcote came to school and fixed the covers to the ink wells in the classrooms.'

July 8th 1867 (I)
'Began using our new Infants' School this morning, admitting several little ones.'

December 13th 1875 (B)
'The playground during this wet weather is almost like a plough field. This, in spite of all efforts, keeps the school floor plastered with mud and the boys' clothes very dirty.'

April 2nd 1884 (B)
'H.M. Inspector's report
The light is poor and I note that half the room is stone paved.'

April 4th 1884 (B)
'I have put a new rope to the school bell so it may be rung to call boys to school in time.'

October 3rd 1884 (B)
'A new porch and entrance to the second classroom was opened this week.'

April 6th 1892 (B)
'Inspector says: the room is insufficiently warmed. A stove seems to be necessary. New desks are needed.'

September 12th 1892 (B)
'The school work was greatly interfered with on account of putting on a new roof.'

September 30th 1892 (B)
'The new roof was finished today.'

April 1893 (B)
'From the Inspector's report:
The diamond panes are not suitable for school purposes and should be replaced by ordinary glazing. The offices (toilets) are not sufficient. The playground should be properly levelled, gravelled and fenced. The defects noticed should be at once remedied.'

April 9th 1897 (B)
'The new offices (toilets) were finished this week.'

July 29th 1897 (B)
'The last lessons in the afternoon have been utilised by having the weeds pulled up in the playground.'

The diamond panes let little natural light in to the school.

December 6th 1898 (B)
'The room has been very dark this afternoon. It is practically impossible to see at one end of the room without having the door open.'

May 1899 (B)
'HMI report
The proper lighting for the room has not yet been attended to, nor has a cupboard for books been supplied. Painting and small repairs are needed. The defects in the lighting must be corrected at once. The Board of Education will expect to be informed that this has been done.'

October 24th 1899 (G)
'HMI Inspector's visit. He advised the removal of some sacred pictures to make room for more maps which he thought should be hung up in the room to be always in sight of the children. The pictures could still be hung in a spare place on the wall.'

December 15th 1899 (B)
'The room was bitterly cold this week. Not withstanding good fires the thermometer never registered beyond 55° and in the mornings it stood at less than 40°.'

November 18th 1901 (G)
'A dense smoke escaping from the classroom stove this morning so filled all the rooms that the children could not come in till it was clear which was about 9.20. Consequently no Bible lesson was given but the whole school learnt the words of a hymn together.'

September 15th 1902 (B)
'The schoolrooms have been cleaned and the walls re-coloured and the yard partly gravelled.'

September 22nd 1902 (B)
'Letter received from the Board of Education stating that the Boys' and Girls' School will in future be known as the Hursley National School.'

This change meant that schools were now funded through the rates.

April 22nd 1903 (B)
'HMI Report states that 'there is no water supply on the premises.' '

May 7th 1903 (G)
'Unpacked some new books and apparatus from the National Society's Depot. Sand trays, ball-frames and coloured laths for Infants – wands for the girls' Drill Exercises – and reading books.'

October 1st 1903 (G)
'From this date the school is taken over by the Hants County Council under new management.

The inventory of school furniture and books included:
54 slates, 23 desks with seats and metal frames, 5 desks without seats, wooden frames, 4 forms, 3 easels, 4 blackboards, 4 doz. wands, 1 teachers table, 4 chairs, 1 piano, 1 harmonium, 1 museum cupboard, 4 fenders, 4 fireguards, 2 pairs tongs, 1 shovel, 1 claw hammer, 1 secular print, 4 wall maps, 3 framed portraits, 1 framed text, 3 photographs of school groups, 1 coal scuttle, 1 pail.

Books included:
Pictures of English History 12 copies – well worn
Making of the Home – 23 copies
Girls at Home – 16 copies
Geography Reader – 24 copies
Historical Reader – 18 copies
Bibles 20 – much worn
Scripture Readers – 30'

March 18ᵗʰ 1904 (B)
'Received two new desks.'

March 18ᵗʰ 1904 (G)
'The playground, which was spread with gravel in the early part of February has just become flat and in good condition. Up to this time it has been in a most sloppy state. A new fence, or rather a mended one, has also been put around it.'

March 25ᵗʰ 1904 (B)
'Received a pedestal desk.
An improvement has been made by fixing a basin in the classroom and water has been laid on the premises.'

April 12ᵗʰ 1904 (B)
'A new grate has been put in and a tortoise stove removed, having been a source of great discomfort through smoke. Water has also been laid on with an outside and inside tap, basin, etc.'

April 15ᵗʰ 1904 (B)
'The school has been much improved in the Easter holidays and no doubt the work will be much better and the comfort of the scholars much more satisfactory.'

July 11ᵗʰ 1904 (B)
'The new partition is a great improvement. However, more light must be provided in the divided portion of the room now used by Standard 1 before the dark days of winter. The ventilation of the whole building is imperfect. A school clock is needed.'

October 14ᵗʰ 1904 (B)
'Received a supply of coal.'

December 15th 1904 (B)
'No drill took place today on account of the bad state of the playground.'

December 5th 1905 (B)
'Difficulty in finishing work on account of lack of light from one side of the school.'

From September to November 1906 (B)
'The noise of the workmen is a serious hindrance to progress.'

January 7th 1907 (N)
'School reopened as a mixed school. There are not sufficient reading books and other material for the combined use of both departments.
The rooms are full and there is no floor space, which makes marching in and out very difficult if not an impossibility.
The playground would be much improved by a coating of gravel, particularly near the school and the hedge.'

February 4th 1907 (N)
'HMI report
The organisation of this school is not good. On each morning the Infants' teacher, Miss Flower, has to take the Arithmetic lesson of Class 2. During these times her class is taught by two of the schoolgirls, neither of which is fourteen years of age. They are therefore, illegally employed.
The boys and girls have a common playground, facing the boys' offices (toilets) screened only by an open railing. The boys can be plainly seen, not only when entering and leaving the closets but when they are using the urinals, a side view of the lads being presented. This should be remedied.

Staff – Samuel Argyle, Edith Lily Flower, Matilda Westbrook.'

March 4th 1907 (N)
'School Managers' Meeting
The children are not to be taken to Church 'as a school.' If they go, consent must first be ascertained from the Local Education Committee and the specified days thus approved must be entered into the timetable. Even then, the church going must be purely voluntary.
A flagstaff flying the Union Jack is to be erected in the school playground.'

September 30th 1912 (N)
'School piano from County Council received today.'

November 24th 1915 (N)
'Nine tons of school coal brought.'

May 25th 1922 (N)
'School library started (30 vols).'

January 8th 1923 (N)
'During the Christmas holidays, rats entered 3 of the cupboards and destroyed many books.'

May 8th 1924 (N)
'Request for fresh supply of peat moss for offices (toilets) forwarded.'

November 19th 1924 (N)
'Two lamps have been provided for the main room and classroom.'

This is the first reference to any artificial lighting in school.

January 7th 1925 (N)
'Seed order for school garden – potatoes, beet, carrot, parsnip, turnip, broad beans, peas, onions, shallots, cabbage, brussels sprouts, broccoli, radish.'

January 26th 1925 (N)
'An oil stove has been provided for the Infant room during the winter – 2½ gallons a week.'

March 5th 1925 (N)
'Rats have again entered Class 2 cupboard destroying team colours and damaging many books – reported to Correspondent.'

September 7th 1925 (N)
'HMI report
Work in this school is much hampered by the unsatisfactory state of the building. In the main room two teachers work under very difficult conditions. The room is dark, ill ventilated and crowded.'

January 24th 1926 (N)
'The playground has been too wet to take drill during past fortnight.'

June 16th 1926 (N)
'Mr Moyce – County Horticultural Expert inspected the gardens.'

November 12th 1926 (N)
'Reported to Correspondent, roof of cookery hut leaking badly.'

June 21st 1927 (N)
'School closed all day. Unveiling of memorial tablet to John Keble in the new school.'

October 4th 1927 (N)
'Removal of furniture and stock to new building commenced today.'

October 12th 1927 (N)
'Moved children and remaining stock into new building.'

October 13th 1927 (JK)
'Vicar opened school.'

November 21ˢᵗ 1927 (JK)
'Reported to Correspondent that owing to water in the cellar it is impossible to light fires.'

January 24ᵗʰ 1928 (JK)
'Very wet day. The path to the school is under water.'

January 30ᵗʰ 1928 (JK)
'It was found impossible to light the furnace as there was 2" of water in the furnace room.'

March 12ᵗʰ 1928 (JK)
'Today received intimation from the Correspondent that the managers, while realising the work and thought given to the laying out of the lawn, flower beds, sunken rock garden and pool, are of the opinion that the grass should be restored and the rock garden removed to the north side of the school. This will entail the giving up of the Class gardens which the children had as their own and for which they had supplied bulbs, flowers, etc. at their own expense.'

March 28ᵗʰ 1928 (JK)
'Reported to Correspondent need for cess-pit being emptied and children from Farley arrived late this morning.'

April 20ᵗʰ 1928 (JK)
'Thirteen trees planted in the playground against the offices (toilets), estate workers doing the job.'

January 18ᵗʰ 1929 (JK)
'Arrangements have been made with Miss Kingsgate of Hursley Village Library to have about 3 dozen books transferred to school. This arrangement may inculcate a love of reading in the children.
A branch of the National Savings has been reformed in school.
Small amounts from 1/2d upwards may be saved at a time, more suitable for children's use.'

February 11ᵗʰ 1929 (JK)
'Bitterly cold morning. No fire. Temperature below 40° in school.'

February 12ᵗʰ 1929 (JK)
'Head with boys' assistance lit stokehole fire.'

February 12ᵗʰ 1931 (JK)
'Report on Gardening Instruction
A good deal of experimental work is carried out. In addition to vegetables, flowers are grown and a number of varieties of strawberries have been planted for trial.'

October 24ᵗʰ 1932 (JK)
'Milk Club began this week. 48 children from Wednesday.'

The government was concerned about the poor nutritional health of children. In 1921 the Free School Milk act allowed, but did not compel, Local Education Authorities to provide 1/3 of a pint of free school milk for those who would like it. In 1946 this was introduced for all children but provision ceased in 1971.

July 11ᵗʰ 1934 (JK)
'For weeks a stench of urine has been noticeable on the school path. This has been attributed to the heat and the position of the girls' lavatories, though on nearly every occasion, the wind was E.N.E and the stench unexplained. Investigation proved that the bucket of urine had been emptied in the bushes on the path side where children brushed against it on entering the school. Man responsible sent for.'

October 20ᵗʰ 1938 (JK)
'First class room being used for the ceremony of switching on the newly installed electric light.'

March 3ʳᵈ 1944 (JK)
'Fire out in stokehole. This is the ninth time since Xmas that the HT has had to leave class and light stokehole fire.'

Alan Rodbourne remembers helping Mr Toyer to light the fire in the stokehole.

'There was a boiler in the cellar and we used to go down and see to it. There was an old boy came along and lit it in the morning about an hour before school started and then in the day we used to have to take turns to keep it going. They used to tip the coke down the chute.'

May 30th 1947 (JK)
'Visit of rodent officer to clear school area.'

September 17th 1947 (JK)
'Telephone now installed –Tel no. Hursley 41.'

Interestingly, the number today is 775 241.

October 24th 1947 (JK)
'School boiler taken to pieces. It will need at least front and back sections renewed.'

December 10th 1948 (JK)
'Condition of schoolyard has rapidly deteriorated during the past year and in wet weather a puddle covers most of the yard. Children falling are in such a mess that clothes are damaged.'

The stone steps leading down to the murky depths of the stokehole.

January 23rd 1953 (JK)
'Boiler fire out. Temperature outside at 9 a.m. 33°. Headmaster spent till 10.30 a.m. lighting and attending to fire.'

April 27th 1953 (JK)
'Piano was tuned during the holiday. Tuner remarked on damage being done by the mice.'

July 24th 1953 (JK)
'This afternoon we held a Bring and Buy sale among the children to raise money to buy a wireless set. We collected £6 10s. 8d.'

December 9th 1954 (JK)
'The clerk of the works called to see the flooded state of the stokehole – water at least 18" deep and pouring down the wall.'

May 2ⁿᵈ 1955 (JK)
'The blackboards have been secured as 1 fell at end of term, fortunately without causing any bodily harm.'

March 6ᵗʰ 1956 (JK)
'Canon Jendwine called to study plans for proposed dining hall and kitchen.'

January 15ᵗʰ 1957 (JK)
'Two representatives from Roads and Bridges came to see the bad state of the playground.'

July 2ⁿᵈ 1957 (JK)
'Miss Kitching came to measure position for climbing apparatus which is on order.'

July 2ⁿᵈ 1958 (JK)
' 'Banda' duplicating machine delivered.'

September 18ᵗʰ 1958 (JK)
'Representative called to examine boiler. Impossible owing to water in stokehole.'

Martyn Welch, brother of the author and a pupil at the school from 1953-1959, tells us more about the problem of the flooded stokehole.

'The stokehole (cellar where the boiler and Mr Smith resided) was prone to flooding. I can still see the water level, shimmering black and brooding as it lapped at the edges of the upper steps. Iron railings disappeared beneath the murky waters and frightened me as though beckoning me down to the waiting depths. There was usually an accompanying strong acrid smell of wet coke which burned the back of my throat, so I always tried to hold my breath as I walked by and averted my gaze.'

October 21st 1958 (JK)
'Piece of ceiling in Class 2 fell down.'

November 17th 1958 (JK)
'We began to use boys' water closets today. Screen temporarily erected round latrine.'

January 12th 1960 (JK)
'Mr Nash called to see land which is to become a school playing field.'

February 4th 1960 (JK)
'Two gentlemen from the Office called re – carpet and curtains for the staff room.'

June 23rd 1960 (JK)
'Lightening strike on boiler plug in kitchen put power out of action.'

September 6th 1960 (JK)
'During the holidays the work of building the kitchen has begun. The netball court has been marked out.'

October 10th 1960 (JK)
'Stokehole much flooded. Cleared by dinnertime so fire could be lit.'

October 28th 1960 (JK)
'Mr Stephens, clerk of the works, called to investigate the matter of the frequent emptying of cesspits necessitated by the unusual heavy rainfall.'

October 3rd 1961 (JK)
'Television delivered.'

May 9th 1962 (JK)
'During the holidays the playground on the north side has been replanned and resurfaced.'

January 9th 1963 (JK)
'Heating has been on since December 24th because of severe freezing. The toilets are usable provided they are flushed with buckets of water.'

March 5th 1963 (JK)
'Sewing machine overhauled by Singer representative.'

November 26th 1963 (JK)
'Hampshire Contractors called re – smelly drains. Nothing can be done at present.'

22

Semolina, pigswill and a washing up shed

I N 1944 the Education Act stated that meals must be provided in all schools. Free meals were available for children from low-income families but everyone else would pay sufficient to cover the cost of the ingredients.

In many schools it wasn't possible to cook on the premises so kitchens were added later, where practical. Until then, meals were driven from a School Meals Cooking Centre to be dished up at school, using the school desks as 'dining tables' if necessary.

October 13th 1941 (JK)
'Circular to parents on school meals drawn up and cyclostyled.'

Cyclostyling was an early form of duplicating documents. Ink was forced through tiny holes in a wax paper stencil to produce multiple copies. This method is now obsolete.

June 1st 1943 (JK)
'Visit of Mrs Jupe re – provision of school dinners.'

June 7th 1943 (JK)
'Visit of architect from the Castle to measure up for shed to do 'washing up', in connection with school dinners.'

November 17th 1943 (JK)
'Second consignment of school dinner equipment was unpacked and checked.'

June 21st 1944 (JK)
'School dinners commenced today. 126 children had dinner. Mrs Kew and Miss D. Freemantle were 'Washers up'.'

July 14th 1944 (JK)
'Dinners did not arrive until 12.50 owing to convoys on the route.'

August 28th 1944 (JK)
'Today the quantity provided (school dinners) was less than ever. Rice pudding was so short that 1 ladle had to serve 3 or 4. Forty-nine children asked for more meat and vegetables and every child asked for more pudding. Neither could be provided.'

February 5th 1945 (JK)
'Mrs Shorto had to take her car to bring forty-four school dinners from Chandler's Ford depot as the depot's phone was out of order and extra dinners could not be ordered.'

September 8th 1947 (JK)
'Owing to suspected food poisoning last week no school dinners are being sent out from Chandler's Ford Cooking Centre this week. Children are to bring their own lunches or go home at noon.'

March 2nd 1953 (JK)
'Increase in price of school dinners from today. Numbers taking them dropped from 80-90 to 50-60. About 1/3 decrease.'

January 18th 1956 (JK)
'Nurse Watson called to follow up re – children not being given dinner money or sandwiches.'

May 6th 1957 (JK)
'We began to have dinners from Romsey Cooking Depot.'

October 21st 1960 (JK)
'Miss Gregory, School Meals Supervisor, called to discuss advertisements for vacancies in new kitchen.'

November 11th 1960 (JK)
'Interviewed applicants for posts of cook and general helper in the school kitchen to be opened after Christmas. Mrs Blake was chosen as cook and Mrs Heath as general helper.'

Martyn Welch paints a lurid picture of his experiences with the pigswill bin –

'We took it in turns to peer into the large aluminium pigswill bin, located near the boys' outside toilet block. These bins contained a pink, (always pink) glutinous mess that was school dinner remains. The pink colour was probably generated by the semolina puddings that none of us liked. The reason for clambering up to endure this ritual was to see how long you could look at the contents and smell the sickly sweet cloying odour before it turned your stomach and made you violently ill – into the bin. The trick was to look away before you reached that dreaded point of no return.'

23

Meet Mabel, Minnie and Maud

FROM small beginnings, seventeen scholars in 1863, the numbers varied throughout the years. In May 1920, Mr Toyer faced all eighty-eight children single handed due to staff absences. By 1954 the number of pupils was around one hundred and thirty.

May 18ᵗʰ 1863 (G)
'Taught almost entirely collectively, having only seventeen children.'

July 29ᵗʰ 1867 (G)
'35 pupils at this time.'

June 1871 (GI)
'62 in school, 23 Infants.'

March 15ᵗʰ 1882 (GI)
'Number on books 41.

Standard I

Sarah Smith	Jessie Alder	Alice Bunney	Jane Self
Lily Flower	Mary Hail	Lottie Callan	Harry Westbrook
Emily Webb	Frederick Chalk	Edith Richards	James Cooper
Mary Nash			

Standard II

F. Bailey	Rose Chalk	Emily Richards	Ena Bradley
Fanny Earle	Mary Down	Frances Hancock	Lily Clark
Florence Alder	Mary Wild		

Standard III

| Mabel Flower | Emma Butter | Elizabeth Hawkins | Maude Bunce |
| Minnie Corbin | Florence Chalk | | |

Standard IV

| Laura Wilson | Cecilia Discombe | Annie Gale | Florence Clark |
| Elizabeth Alder | Sophia Whitmash | | |

Standard V

| Mary Cooper | Mary Weeks | Kate Churcher |

Standard VI

| Florence Wilson | Emily Elkins | Agnes Jones |

October 8th 1888 (B)
'51 present.'

April 2nd 1906 (B)
'50 on roll.'

April 9th 1907 (N)
'In Standards 3 to 7 there are 64 children which I have to teach unaided. The work is hampered and crippled under such conditions.'

March 30th 1911 (N)
'134 present.'

March 6th 1912 (N)
'137 present.'

November 12th 1917 (N)
'I am working with 77 children in 5 Standards with an overcrowded room, and seating for 68.'

May 16th 1920 (N)
'I have charge of 88 Standards III-VII single handed.'

Hursley Scouts in 1911.

Standard IV in 1928.

January 7th 1926 (N)
'Numbers on books 109.'

April 12th 1926 (N)
'116 on books.
Miss Laidman absent. 78 children taken in main room by Headmaster.'

May 5th 1941 (JK)
'154 on books.'

May 1st 1950 (JK)
'Numbers 148.'

January 7th 1952 (JK)
'156 on books.'

March 12th 1952 (JK)
'After the decapitation of the school and transfer of all seniors to Winchester Secondary Modern schools, the staff, with the exception of the teacher of the seniors, will remain. The approx numbers of the school, consisting of Infants and Juniors to 11+ will be 100-124.
The school will be divided into 4 classes.'

December 19th 1952 (JK)
'All children over 11+ left the school today. Boys to attend the new Secondary Modern School, Romsey Road, girls to attend Danemark School (Winchester) on Jan 3rd 1953.'

January 5th 1953 (PS)
'School has now become a definite Primary School instead of an 'All Standard' one.'

Children now left Primary School at eleven years old and moved on to secondary schools, whereas previously they remained in the 'All Standard' school until they were twelve or thirteen, when they could leave.

And finally...

MANY pupils have passed through the Hursley Schools since records began in 1863, all with very different needs and backgrounds. Estate workers' children, workhouse residents, May Queens, truants, Morris dancers, choir members and sports teams.

Between them, they lived through many historic changes, including several monarchs, two World Wars, and the coming of motor transport. From slates to computers, from the excitement of seeing a pure white mole to the TV footage of the shooting of an American president, all were milestones in the lives of yesterday's children.

Most important of all, what the pupils have in common to this day, is the inspiration, care and skills of all the teachers and head teachers, who tell their story, through the entries in the logbooks.

Their dedication will not be forgotten. We will remember them, every one.

Thank you . . .

My thanks go to everyone listed below –

- Len D Peach for allowing me to include many of his Hursley postcard collection, for the gift of his book 'Merdone' and for taking time to help me uncover background facts,

- Cicely Bull, Alan Rodbourne and Martyn Welch for sharing their colourful anecdotes,

- Helen Hart for help with editing,

- Hilary Jane Wells, photographer extraordinaire, for patiently walking round the village with me, taking pictures,

- Karen Morgan and Hilary Jane Wells for designing and photographing the cover,

- The head teacher, teachers and administrative staff at John Keble School for their invaluable help, encouragement and support.

Bibliography

I am very grateful for the use of information from the following sources –

Hursley 2000 A Collection of Memories   Stan Rawdon 2000

Merdone, the history of Hursley Park   D Len Peach 1978

The Hursley Hunt   William Scarth-Dixon 1927

Without the use of the Internet I could not have found the historical details to set the logbook extracts in their context. There's not room here to list every web site I used but I do want to mention Peter Higginbotham's site about the history of the workhouse. Further fascinating facts about workhouse life may be found at http://www.workhouses.org